Surviving a Wilderness Emergency

OutdoorSafe Press
Colorado Springs, Colorado

Surviving a Wilderness Emergency

Practical advice on what to do when you find yourself in trouble in the backcountry

Peter Kummerfeldt

Published by:
OutdoorSafe Press
6612 Frederick Drive
Colorado Springs, CO 80918
www.outdoorsafe.com
email: info@outdoorsafe.com
Phone: 719-593-5852

ISBN - 10: 0-9776459-0-8
ISBN - 13: 978-0-9776459-0-9

Library of Congress Control Number: 2005938903

Printed in the United States of America

March 2006

10 9 8 7 6 5 4

WARNING

The information provided herein is designed for educational use only and is not a substitute for specific training or experience. The author has made every effort to ensure the information was correct at the time of publication. OutdoorSafe, Inc., and the author assume no liability for any individual's use of or reliance upon any material contained or referenced herein. Further, the author disclaims any liability to any party for whichever losses or damage caused by errors, omissions, misleading information that may occur. When going outdoors it is the reader's responsibility to have the proper knowledge, experience and equipment to travel safely.

DEDICATION

This book is dedicated to all the military men and women who have given their lives not only in defense of the United States but also many other countries - countries that now live in freedom because of their sacrifice. It is also dedicated to those who did not return from foreign shores. They too are remembered.

ACKNOWLEDGMENTS

Publishing of this book would not have been possible without the assistance of many people, not the least of whom was my wife, Mary Kummerfeldt, who pushed, cajoled, coaxed, twisted my arm, encouraged and finally sat back in relief when the manuscript went to the printers. As the person behind the exhibit booth at endless conferences, sport shows and other venues, she was the one that had to answer the frequently asked question, "When is he going to write a book?" Now she can hand them one!

My appreciation is also expressed to the following people for their assistance in the development, review and editing of this manual.

Virginia Anderson, an author of many books, who volunteered her time to edit an early version of the book and provided much valuable input on the grammar and the organization of the material.

Skip Stoffel, Rich Lahn, Ralph Wilfong and Mike Baird for their technical input and the constructive criticism they gave me on the content of the book.

Melissa Anderson for the time she took to get me started in digital photography and Adobe Photoshop. The production of all the photographs used in this text would not have been possible without her assistance.

Finally, I would like to acknowledge the lessons I have learned from those who attended my seminars and then found themselves in an emergency. Their experiences served to validate the survival principles, procedures and skills that are included in ***Surviving a Wilderness Emergency.***

TABLE OF CONTENTS

FOREWORD

I'm not sure where I met Peter Kummerfeldt. His name is such a household word, that our initial meeting escapes me, possibly because I feel like I've known him for a long, long time. My most vivid memory of Peter was at an outdoor workshop sponsored by Safari Club International at a camp in Wyoming. I remember being absolutely spellbound as I watched Peter discuss survival techniques. His presentation was so amazingly thought-provoking that I knew that I was listening to a man who is truly a master, a person who had been there and done that.

Peter is not a Johnny-come-lately in the outdoors. He paid his dues. With 30 years of experience in The U.S. Air Force, where he worked as a survival instructor in the Arctic Survival School in Alaska, and the Jungle Survival School in the Philippines, he is truly an expert in every sense of the word. This is a man who has tested himself around the world, and met those challenges, passing on his wisdom to those of us who have no such experiences.

I remember listening to Peter as he talked about little details that we'd never give a second thought to - like what kinds of specific matches to use if our life depended on a warming fire. And how to signal for help if we were lost, and how to improvise if we found ourselves in a situation where Mother Nature could kill us if we didn't know how to meet the challenges - profound challenges that meant life or death.

In this book, Peter spares no details. He addresses every aspect of survival, from the psychological elements of dealing with our brain when we comprehend that we need help, to the gear we need to bring along to prevent us from injury when we find ourselves indeed lost, and to the very basic knowledge we'll need to overcome that very terrifying ordeal when we find ourselves in a survival situation.

I've spent all my adult life in the outdoors. I have two degrees in forestry and wildlife, and worked as a forest ranger and wildlife biologist for 15 years. In 1978 I joined Outdoor Life as a full time staff hunting writer. In that capacity, the mountains, deserts and prairies have been my workplace. I thought I knew a little something about the outdoors, but then I met Peter Kummerfeldt, and was amazed at what I didn't know. I still listen to Peter, always learning something new, and I'm profoundly satisfied that he has now put his wisdom into this book.

Don't read this book once. Read it as many times as necessary to absorb the information within. And don't be so smug as to believe a survival ordeal can't happen to you. If you spend time in the outdoors, whether you're an angler, hunter, photographer, hiker, or whatever, you could find yourself in a life-threatening situation. Complacency and ignorance can kill you. Be informed. Digest everything in this book, and remember that mother nature is not always a lady. When she's at her worst, she is a witch, and she will destroy you with incredible ease. Prepare yourself to fight back. Trust Peter's words of wisdom, and you'll be forever thankful if you ever meet a survival situation head on. Every year, people are transported out of the woods in a body bag. A terribly morbid thought, I know, but its reality. Be a survivor. Take Peter's words to heart. One day, you may be glad you did.

Jim Zumbo, Hunting Editor
Outdoor Life Magazine

INTRODUCTION

Surviving a wilderness emergency begins with a recognition that somewhere, sometime in the future you might have to spend an unplanned (not unexpected) night or two out in the backcountry. Unfortunately, the majority of people believe that it will always be someone else who is in this predicament. Someone else who is thrown from a horse; someone else who becomes the lone survivor of an aircraft accident; someone else whose car slides off of the road and the occupants end up having to survive in the car until they are rescued; someone else who gets lost after following a wounded animal into unfamiliar country. That "someone else" is in fact each one of us! Survival experiences can occur anywhere and often occur when we least expect to find ourselves in trouble – when we are least prepared to cope!

There are many scenarios that could result in a person having to survive a night or two in the open. Becoming lost is often the catalyst that begins a chain of events that result in you having to practice your survival skills. Inclement weather may force you to hole-up for the night. Illness or injury may cause you to have to stay-put until rescue comes. You can find yourself stranded when bad weather prevents you from being picked up at the appointed time. Traveling on foot after dark is dangerous and, while the urge to be back in camp with your buddies is very strong, it is usually safer to bivouac for the night. Faced with any one of these situations you must now "survive" for an indefinite period of time – it may only be a few hours until the sun comes up or the weather clears or several days could elapse before the rescuers locate and rescue you.

What does it take to survive? What does the word "survival" mean? Why do some people survive and yet others die in similar situations? What kind of preparation is needed for an "unplanned night out?" This manual will answer these questions and many more.

The purpose of this manual is to:

- Heighten the reader's awareness of potentially life-threatening hazards and thereby reduce the number of injuries and fatalities occurring in the backcountry.

- Motivate the readers to better clothe and equip themselves so that, when confronted with a night out, the situation does not become life threatening - just inconvenient.

- Teach the readers practical survival skills NOT primitive skills! While primitive skills such as fire-by-friction have their place, few people will devote the necessary time to become proficient in these skills.

My point of departure for the material contained in this manual will be the belief that no one is more concerned about your safety than you should be and that, while we would like to believe that there will always be someone to help us, many times there isn't. Don't depend on others – carry your own emergency equipment, learn how to shelter yourself, to build your own fire, to affect your own rescue! We would also like to believe that we will be unhurt as we begin our survival experience – often this is not the case and we find that normally simple tasks are infinitely more difficult to accomplish. (Try zipping up your jacket with one hand!)

This manual is not intended to address the needs of someone who is living in a remote part of the world for an indefinite period of time.

Rather, it is intended to help the inexperienced individual who finds himself or herself having to spend an unplanned night out.

There are many "how-to-survive" books and manuals in and out of print available to anyone interested in increasing their knowledge of surviving a wilderness emergency. Few of these sources are directed at the hiker, skier, hunter, bird watcher, etc. who gets lost and has to spend an uncomfortable night out waiting for the sun to come up. They are more commonly directed at long-term survival in some remote corner of the world. Additionally, the information presented in these books is of little practical value to the average man or woman who is unlikely to have practiced the skills illustrated in these books to the point that the skills can be relied upon in an emergency. You can't live off the land! You must bring with you what you need to survive. To that end, this manual attempts to provide practical guidance on the steps that need to be taken to survive a night or two out, under adverse conditions, until those conditions abate or the people involved are rescued.

One final thought. Reading this manual is a good start to your preparations but there is no substitute for practicing the skills.

1

Defining The Word "Survival"

"Survival is an attitude."

The word "survival" conjures up a Hollywood picture of some horrendous situation that takes place in a remote part of the world where the "survivor" has to "survive" under extreme conditions, without food, with only limited (or no) water while fending off the onslaught of predatory animals! Let's get real. While some survival experiences do occur in such places, many more occur in the woodlots of Wisconsin, when duck hunting in Louisiana, or while tracking deer in Washington – in short, anywhere we recreate or work in the outdoors.

There are many book definitions of the word "survival," but none adequately describe the difficulties in which people sometimes find themselves.

Here's my definition:

SURVIVAL: *The ability and the desire to stay alive, all alone, under adverse conditions, until rescued.*

• ***Ability*** - These are skills in which you need to become proficient if you expect to survive: first aid, sheltering, fire craft, water procurement, and signaling. Without these skills, your survival may depend largely on luck. These are skills that cannot be learned "on the job," but must be practiced ahead of time so that when the emergency arises, you can shelter yourself, build a fire, procure water, and construct signals in minimum time and with a minimum amount of expended effort.

• ***Desire*** - You must want to survive! You must want to live! Without the desire to live, it doesn't matter how much equipment or training you have. There have been survivors who lacked even the minimum amount of equipment, who had never received any survival training but who had a tremendous tenacity to live – and they did! There have also been people who were trained and equipped but lacked the will to survive who died when they should have lived!

Survivors, who are inadequately clothed and poorly equipped as well as those who have never practiced their survival skills will have their "desire to live" severely tested. On the other hand, those who can stay warm and dry, those who have equipped themselves, and those who have practiced their survival skills may experience an uncomfortable night or two out, but because of their preparations, they should not find themselves in a life-threatening emergency.

• ***Stay alive -*** First of all, staying alive means being able to administer first aid – to yourself! Few people begin their survival situations uninjured! Few people in survival situations remain uninjured! Any injuries that are incurred during or following an accident must be dealt with quickly -- you will be both the patient and the doctor! When was the last time you attended a First Aid course? Could you administer effective CPR to a drowning or lightning strike victim? Would those with whom you travel know what to do if you were the one that needed help?

In a cold, wet, windy environment, staying alive means keeping warm; in a hot environment, staying cool is the objective. Accomplishing either can be very difficult. *98.6° F* is the most important number in your life! A deviation of 5° F above or below 98.6° F significantly impairs your brain's ability to function and reduces your ability to make good decisions. Since surviving is largely a "decision making" process, your brain's ability to function must be protected at all costs.

Staying alive also means keeping yourself hydrated. Every physiological activity that takes place in the human body takes place in a water environment. When that water is depleted, those activities begin to malfunction. Under stressful conditions, dehydrated people quickly lose their working efficiency and, worse than that, their ability to think clearly and make good decisions!

• ***Under adverse conditions*** **-** Because of our past experiences, what may be adverse to one person may be routine to another. A person growing up in North Dakota might find that spending a night out in a Louisiana swamp is an adverse experience! A Cajun who was raised in those swamps would find trying to survive a northern blizzard equally uncomfortable. Those environments which we are familiar with we are not intimidated by, but when taken out of our comfort zone and placed in a totally unfamiliar environment the situation can become adverse very quickly!

• ***All alone*** **-** Never count on anyone else being there to help you when you are in trouble. If there is another person, you can pool your talents, your equipment and clothing for the benefit of all. But if there is no one, and you have never developed your survival skills because you said to yourself, "Someone else (husband, father, mother, brother, sister, guide etc.) will take care of me," you have just fallen into a big trap. You will be totally unprepared physically and psychologically! Plan on being alone!

• ***Until rescued*** **-** Beyond readying the appropriate signals to attract the attention of rescuers, there is little the survivor can do to expedite the rescue process. Finding an overdue hunter, backpacker or birdwatcher takes time – especially if you have failed to leave a flight plan! To the survivor, the time it takes to be found and recovered seems to drag on forever; and remaining in one place waiting to be found and rescued will take all of your willpower. History shows that those survivors who were able to overcome their impatience and desire to walk out had a better chance of surviving than those that continued to move. Sit tight, survive and wait for rescue to come to you.

2

Survival Myths And Misconceptions

"Surviving a near death experience does not make you a survivor. It makes you damn lucky!"

Much of the information available to people who want to learn more about survival and surviving is based on material that is outdated and often totally incorrect. Unfortunately early outdoor writers have created a problem for those interested in learning how to survive a wilderness emergency today. Techniques and procedures that were once state-of-the-art are no longer valid. Some of what was once thought of as an appropriate method is now not only inappropriate but in some cases dangerous.

The times have changed. The needs of a hiker who gets lost today are different from the needs of the mountain men who trapped beaver in the American west and lived off the land while doing so. The individual who gets in trouble today is unlikely to have devoted sufficient time to practicing survival skills, is unlikely to have clothed and equipped him or herself adequately, and, consequently, is unlikely to be able to spend a night out without great discomfort. Skills that were once second nature can no longer be counted on when difficulties arise. Even a once commonplace skill, such as striking a match to light a fire, is no longer commonplace.

Many myths, misconceptions and misunderstandings exist today and, as a result, the inexperienced person, when confronted with a night out in the bush, experiences unnecessary discomfort, hardship, injury and sometimes death because of their reliance on antiquated information and techniques. If you were to open some of the currently available "how-to-survive" books you would find techniques and procedures that date back to those who survived by manufacturing what they needed from the resources on hand.

The question is, "How appropriate are these techniques and procedures today?" In many cases, they are not! However, despite the passing of time, the fact that the advice given is still in printed form implies that the information must still be valid. In many cases it is not. New and better procedures have been developed. Newer equipment is available.

The result of all of this misinformation is that inexperienced people who find themselves in trouble today believe that they can rub sticks together and start a fire. They believe that a waterproof, wind proof shelter can be built from natural materials. They believe that they can live off the land until they are rescued. It must be so – it's in the book!

Many contemporary writers perpetuate the problem. Much of the rubbish that is published in the popular outdoor magazines would never be published if the writer (or the editor) first went out and tested the procedures they write about. Instead, they go to their bookshelf, remove a survival or woods lore book written a hundred years ago, extract from it some procedure used by Jim Bridger to build a fire and present it once again as if the procedure is still valid today. Sometimes it is but most often it is not!

More confusion results from the contemporary experiences of those who survived traumatic incidents. They quickly become the newest "survival expert!" They survived, therefore, what they did to survive must be valid! Sometimes it is and sometimes it isn't. Sometimes people survive despite what they did. They got lucky!

The following is a short discussion of some of the more blatant myths and misconceptions commonly found in print today.

Firecraft. Building and maintaining a fire is fundamental to survival. If you were to believe the advice given in most survival literature, the ability to produce heat and light is an easy one. Simply rub sticks together and, presto, you have fire. Nothing can be further from the truth. Without considerable practice and prior preparation, producing fire by rubbing sticks together is very difficult! Even with practice and preparation, starting a fire by rubbing sticks together can be difficult! When fire-by-friction was the primary way to produce a fire, the necessary equipment was carried by the user much as we today would carry a BIC® lighter or a match.

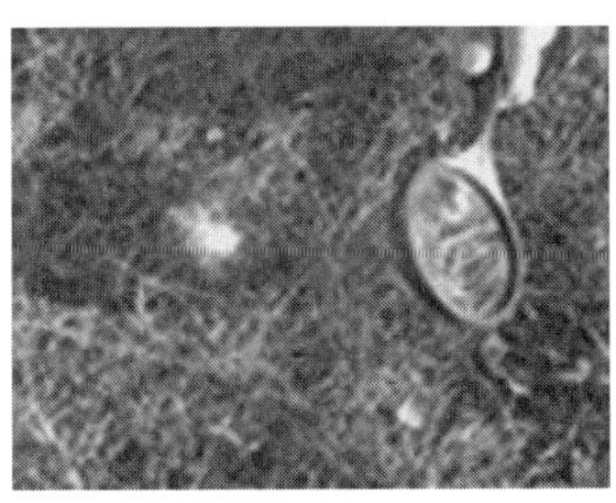

The use of a magnifying lens is another fire starting method that is more myth than reality. The writers of the articles would have you believe that tinder can be ignited using the lens from your eye glasses. Or that you can remove the glass lenses from your camera or binoculars and then, using the lens, focus a beam of sunlight onto the tinder until it ignites. The writers talk of "shaving and shaping a piece of ice into a "lens" and then using it to ignite the tinder! This begs the question "When do you need a fire?" Not on a bright sunny day in the middle of summer, but on a cold, wintry day when the sun is low on the southern horizon or as the sun is about to set or the storm is about to break and your spouse or child is dying from hypothermia! Carrying a magnifying glass to start a fire makes no sense when there are other much more reliable devices that can be depended upon.

Cigarette lighters have often been touted as a piece of equipment that should be carried in your survival kit. Cigarette lighters are difficult to light when your hands have lost their dexterity. They do not perform well under cold conditions or at higher altitudes and, if dropped into a fire accidentally, they explode sending shrapnel in every direction!

Matches come in many forms and to the unknowing they may all look alike. Another trap! What do the words "safety," "strike anywhere," "storm proof," and "waterproof" really mean? In each case there are significant survival ramifications. Chapter 13 will cover fire building in detail.

Sheltering. Here, once again, confusion exists about the kinds of shelters that were built to protect those who ventured into the outdoors to hunt, fish, backpack, etc., and those needed by a survivor. Most survivors first become aware of the need for shelter as it begins to rain or as the sun sets over the western horizon. Most survivors are dehydrated and possibly hypothermic as they begin their survival experience! Some are injured. Could they build a lean-to or debris hut? I doubt it! Building a shelter from natural materials is possible:

- if time allows,
- if the weather conditions permit,
- if there are plenty of natural materials available,
- if the survivor practiced building an emergency shelter previously,
- if cutting tools (knife or saw) are available, and
- if the survivor is uninjured!

But lacking time, skill, natural resources, tools, and the use of both hands, building a windproof, waterproof shelter from natural materials becomes impossible. It is wiser to carry waterproof material with you. Carry large plastic bags that you can crawl into or a tarp to crawl under to protect yourself rather than trying to build one of the many survival shelters shown in the books. Sheltering and shelter building is covered in more detail in Chapter 12.

Signaling. In addition to staying alive, a survivor's greatest need is to be rescued as quickly as possible and to do that you must be able to indicate to others that you are in trouble and need help. Once again the books, manuals and magazine articles are full of nonsense. Three fires placed in a triangle, wetting a slab of wood to form a reflective surface and other labor intensive, less-than-effective procedures are commonly featured in survival literature. With the equipment available today, inexpensive, effective devices are available with which to signal and get rescued quickly. Chapter 14 addresses signaling and rescue procedures.

Survival medicine, defined as the medicine that survivors would administer to themselves or to others that are with them in a wilderness setting, is another area where many myths, misconceptions and misunderstanding exist. Unlike the medical community, who are required to attend Continuing Medical Education training annually, those who recreate or work in the outdoors have no such requirement. Their knowledge of medicine and medical practice is based on first aid courses they may have taken and, once again, on what they read in the popular outdoor press – which may or may not be current. For example, there are those who still believe that "cut and suck" is the standard treatment for a snakebite! Some still think that the treatment for a frostbite injury is to rub the frozen tissue with snow! Still others are reluctant to render aid to a person struck by lightning for fear that they will be electrocuted when they touch the victim! Much confusion exists over how long water should be boiled before it can be consumed safely! The treatment of hypothermia is another area where the knowledge of the non-medical community lags far behind the current standards of practice as advocated by organizations like the Wilderness Medical Society.

Surviving an emergency is difficult but not impossible if the survivor is prepared. That preparation must be based on good information, selecting your clothing and equipment carefully, and practicing your survival skills. Select your "experts" carefully. Read widely and compare the recommendations they give you. What worked for one may or may not work for you. Select procedures and techniques that work under a wide variety of conditions – procedures and techniques that work for you. Just because you are told something works don't accept it until you have tested it in the field.

3

Three Little Words

"Survival is tough, but it's tougher when you're stupid!"

There are many things that get people in trouble when they venture into the outdoors: lack of preparedness, not paying attention to the weather, accidents, etc. More commonly, it is our attitude towards our safety that is the precursor to a life threatening event occurring.

How many times have you said to yourself or have heard others say, *"I am just........."* as in *"I'm just going to walk up the ridge and see if I can see a deer,"* or *"I'm just going to be out for fifteen minutes,"* or perhaps *"I'm just going to run down to the store"*? I believe these three little words, *"I am just,"* get more people into trouble than any other three little words I can think of!

Most commonly, you don't verbalize these words out loud, but say them to yourself, silently, which is even more dangerous. Many times you are not even conscious of your decision to leave your gear behind. Unconsciously, you already have made the decision to leave it because *"I am just ...."* When spoken out loud there is always the chance that someone, upon hearing you say, *"I am just ...."* will step in and remind you of the importance of always taking your emergency clothing and equipment with you even though the possibility of having to spend an unplanned night out is remote.

It is easy to convince yourself that nothing life threatening will happen after all you are *"just ...."* When you use the word "just," you are convincing yourself that the weather will remain pleasant, that no accident will happen, that you will not get lost, and that you will be able to get back before dark! You are saying to yourself that you don't need to carry your daypack with your emergency gear and warm clothing because you won't need it *"you are just ...."*

It is easy to rationalize away the need to always carry your backup clothing and emergency equipment. As the years ago by, one hunting season follows another, and you have yet to spend that unplanned night out, so the temptation to reduce the weight of the daypack you are carrying by leaving your survival kit at home can be very attractive. As you look to the mountains in anticipation of having to ascend on foot and hunt at higher altitudes, it is natural to want to lighten your load and leave behind those pieces of equipment that you have seldom, if ever, used. Sometimes it is "space" or the lack of it which causes you to decide to leave items behind that you should take. Most often, it's the short trips that get you in trouble! After all, *"I was just ...."*

You become complacent. Nothing life threatening ever has happened in the past and so it is easy to convince yourself that it won't happen in the future and if it does you can handle it whatever "it" is! Ignoring the possibility of finding yourself in a survival situation is like playing Russian roulette. Falling victim to the *"I am just"* syndrome is like playing Russian roulette with five out of six chambers loaded!

History is replete with examples of those finding themselves in trouble who, after being rescued from some horrendous situation, said *"I was just ...."* Several years ago in Oregon, an older man left his camp one evening he was *"just"* going to walk down to the end of the ridge and see if he could spot an elk. The following morning was the opening day of elk season. He never returned and, despite an extensive search, he was not found alive. Ten days later his body, partially buried under snow, was discovered by other hunters. His emergency gear consisted of a hunting knife, a compass, a small flashlight and a .357 Magnum pistol. He had tried to shelter himself by drawing the butt ends of two logs together and laying slabs of bark on top of the logs to provide a crude roof. His clothing, a mixture of cotton and wool, failed to provide the protection he needed from the environmental conditions he encountered. Physiologically, he died from hypothermia, but it also could be said that he died because he had rationalized away the need to carry any additional emergency gear. Equipment that he could have used to increase his protection from cold temperatures, precipitation and wind-chill: a big plastic bag or tarp. Equipment that he could have used to attract the attention of the rescuers that were looking for him: a mirror, whistle, survival radio, or 406 MHz emergency beacon. He was *"just going to walk to the end of the ridge, look for an elk and then return to camp!"*

The words *"I am just"* when spoken out loud or silently should be considered a red flag warning! When you say them yourself or hear others say them, STOP! The trap is being set! Continuing on will only spring the trap and once you are in it, there may be no escape. Without adequate clothing, without waterproof sheltering material, without the ability to build a fire or signal to others, survival depends on an individual's tenacity to live, their ability to improvise what they need, and luck – sometimes that's not enough!

4

The Need To Prepare

"Those who are prepared to survive an emergency usually will, while those who are not prepared probably won't!"

Preparation is fundamental to surviving. The need to prepare is motivated by the knowledge that somewhere, sometime, you might have to spend an unplanned night out! Unfortunately, most people won't admit that they might be the ones faced with a life or death situation or some other equally disagreeable circumstance. Denial leads the list of the coping methods that people use - we *deny* anything bad is ever going to happen. It's often easier to *deny* than to prepare for a difficult situation and, as a result, we find ourselves totally unprepared when disaster strikes. It's easy to say, "I'll assemble a survival kit tomorrow." It's easy to rationalize, "I don't have the money to buy a better rain jacket" or "I'll never be in a survival situation." "What do I need a survival kit for?" It's easy to think that it will always be someone else that ends up in a survival situation. Consequently, the vast majority of people upon finding themselves facing a cold night out do so without adequate clothing, without basic survival equipment, and without having practiced building a fire, erecting a shelter or signaling for help.

To prepare, potential survivors need to consider three areas: physical, mental and spiritual preparation.

Physical Preparation

Physical preparation includes carefully selecting your clothing, equipping yourself for an unplanned night out, and getting in better physical condition.

Clothing: What you wear may be adequate to get you to work and back, but will it keep you warm if you have to spend the night in the ditch when your car skids off the road? How much protection will your T-shirt and shorts provide you if you are caught out in a late summer thunderstorm during an afternoon hike? Becoming lost, probably the most common way that people end up "surviving," places a premium on the clothing you are wearing. In the final analysis, the value of your clothing will be determined by its ability to keep you warm and dry when you are inactive!

During the colder, wetter times of the year, dressing properly begins by getting rid of your cotton underwear and switching to synthetics (polypropylene, polyester) or wool. Cotton absorbs the moisture your body produces and holds it against your skin and, as a result, heat will be constantly conducted away. You will never be warm. ***Cotton kills!*** The synthetics are hydrophobic (water hating) and make possible the movement of water vapor away from your body resulting in a layer of dry, warm fabric against your skin.

The next layer, the mid layer, serves to facilitate the movement of water vapor out to the environment and to trap "dead air" around you to keep you warm. Once again, the synthetic fabrics work best - the piles and fleeces - with wool coming in a close second.

Under very cold conditions, an additional insulation layer may be needed. The more "dead air" you trap around you, the warmer you will be. Many insulating materials are available to choose from, both synthetic and natural. I choose synthetics primarily because, unlike many natural fibers, the synthetic insulators do not collapse when wet. Synthetic fabrics are also easier to dry should they become wet, but melt easily when exposed too closely to flame.

The outer layer may be the most important. It must keep the inner layers dry and keep the wind out. If either moisture or wind penetrates the insulation layers, heat will be lost quickly. Studies have shown that in windy situations a good outer shell can increase warmth by as much as fifty percent. Put another way, a good windproof outer layer decreases the amount of insulation needed to keep you warm.

The objective is to use the fewest layers of clothing that will keep you warm when you are *inactive.* Activity generates substantial amounts of body heat and reduces the need for multiple layers of clothing. On the other hand inactivity drives the need to insulate yourself from the environment and to conserve whatever heat your body is producing – very important in a survival situation! Special attention should be paid to protecting your head and your hands. Hands suffer quickly when exposed to cool-to-cold conditions. Fine motor skills, the ability to touch finger to thumb, are lost quickly. Could you zip up your jacket if your fingers are cold and stiff? Could you tie your bootlaces? Gloves and mittens are an important part of your outdoor clothing.

Equipment: Equipping yourself to spend a night out is the next step. There are those that advocate the construction of survival shelters built from natural materials. I disagree. For the average inexperienced person, building a windproof, waterproof shelter from sticks, boughs, bark and other natural materials may be impossible! Shelters built from natural materials take hours to build, require cutting tools and adequate supplies of suitable materials, and, most importantly, call for an "able" survivor - one who is uninjured! Seldom can all of these criteria be met and, for lack of shelter, the survivor ends up spending a very uncomfortable, sometimes life-threatening night or two out. Additionally, inexperienced people will often wait until the sun is about to set or the storm is about to break before they recognize the need for an emergency shelter! I believe that a vital part of your survival equipment is a waterproof, windproof, heavy-duty, plastic bag that you can crawl into! Alternatively, carry a sturdy tarp or piece of plastic that can be quickly erected to create a lean-to or pup tent style of shelter. Chapter 12 provides additional information on emergency shelters.

The ability to ignite a fire may also be critical to your survival. Once again, relying on improvised means, i.e., rubbing sticks together, is an invitation to disaster! Because of injury or loss of finger dexterity due to the cold even the usual methods of starting a fire may become very difficult. How do you strike a match if you only have the use of one hand? Could you still "flick your BIC®" when your fingers are cold and stiff? It can be done, but it won't be easy. Equip yourself with good matches and a metal match. Fill a screw-top match case with cotton balls that have been saturated in Vaseline (Petroleum Jelly) - it makes great tinder, can be ignited with either a match or a spark from the metal match and burns for many minutes.

Improving your physical fitness should be part of the physical preparations you make. Those that are in good physical shape are less likely to injure themselves and those survivors that are injured as a result of an accident will often fare better than those who are not physically fit.

MENTAL PREPARATION

Preparing yourself mentally is as important, if not more so, than preparing yourself physically. If you can't visualize the situations you might find yourself in, it is difficult to know how to prepare for them. Ask yourself two questions: *"What scares me about having to spend an unplanned night out?"* and *"What is the worst thing that can happen to me and am I prepared to cope with it?"* Is it the fear of predatory animals? Starving to death? Dying from hypothermia? Isolation? We all have fears and, unfortunately, these fears are usually not based on good information. Rather, they are based on stories we were told, on TV programs we have watched, or on the books we read. Some of the issues that make us uncomfortable result from the nursery rhymes we were read as children (Little Red Riding Hood, The Three Little Pigs, etc.), the written accounts of other people in trouble, the stories that are told around the campfire, and other tall tales that make the rounds whenever we gather together. Good entertainment perhaps, but often poor sources of reliable information upon which to base your decisions and actions. Make a list – a written list of all of the things that raise your apprehension level. Don't let your ego stand in the way of clearly and specifically identifying those issues that cause you concern. Be brutally honest with yourself. Whether you live or die may be determined by how candid you are when evaluating your knowledge and your skills.

Answering these two questions truthfully is the first step in overcoming one of the biggest barriers to preparing for a future survival situation: denial of the possibility of an emergency happening. If you can see yourself in a survival situation, then preparing for it should naturally follow.

Having made a list, investigate each fear and each phobia, then determine the validity of your anxiety. Go to the experts. Find out the truth. In most instances, you will find that the facts are very different from the fiction and, as a good friend of mine says, *"When you remove the mystery, you'll remove the fear!"*

Spiritual Preparation

Spiritual preparation is the third leg of a three-legged survival stool. Some attention may be appropriate. After reading the accounts of many prisoners-of-war and others who have survived difficult situations, it is clear to me that *"there are no non-believers in survival situations"*! The individuals in these situations may have begun the experience without any strong beliefs one way or the other, but, inevitably, most survivors turned to a greater power for additional help.

As was mentioned at the beginning of this chapter: *"Preparation is fundamental to survival."* Doug Ritter of Equipped to Survive Foundation, Inc., says it even better: *"If you are adequately clothed, if you have equipped yourself and if you have practiced your survival skills, a night or two out should not a be a life threatening experience. On the other hand if you are not clothed adequately, do not have any emergency gear and have never practiced your survival skills whether you survive or not will depend on your will to survive, your ability to improvise, and LUCK."*

I don't know about you, but I want to be clothed, equipped and practiced!

5

What Am I Preparing For?

"Be prepared not scared."

Previous chapters have defined the word *survival* and have discussed the importance of being prepared as opposed to trying to improvise what you need from materials at hand. It is now time to look at some of the situations that people find themselves in where their knowledge of how to survive combined with a basic survival kit and good clothing can bring about a positive ending to their experience or the lack of knowledge, equipment and clothing could result in tragedy.

The question then is *"What am I preparing for?"* As I see it, there are five broad categories that encompass most situations where you may have to survive until rescued or until the weather conditions improve and you can rescue yourself. The categories are:

- becoming lost
- being caught out after dark
- becoming stranded
- becoming ill or injured and unable to proceed
- inclement weather that makes continuing on dangerous

Becoming Lost

If it hasn't happened yet it will sooner or later. Probably more than once! Becoming lost is, in itself, not a critical situation. After all, as someone once said, *"If you like it where you are, you ain't lost!"*

While there are people who appear to be truly gifted in their ability to keep themselves oriented, no one has a "built-in homing device" that enables them to find their way out when the landmarks are obscured by dense timber, bad weather or darkness. Whether we do it consciously or unconsciously, when we travel, we keep ourselves oriented by what we can see and, when we can't see, we must use a compass and a map or Global Positioning System (GPS) receiver to maintain our orientation.

Finding yourself lost can be a terrifying experience. How you react when you discover that you are lost will often determine the eventual outcome of the scenario. When suddenly nothing looks familiar. When the sun is setting in the *east* and the river appears to be flowing *uphill*. **You are lost**! **Admit it!** When you are no longer able to determine which path will lead you back to your truck, the urge to keep moving faster and faster can quickly overcome you. It's easy to convince yourself, "It's just over the next hill" or "the next one" and you keep running! This urge to keep moving must be controlled. Continuing to move makes a bad situation even worse – it increases the risk of injury; increases dehydration; wastes the limited amount of energy you have within you; and, you move further and further away from the last place where you were still "found!"

Sit down! Get off of your feet! **Have a drink – of water!** Drinking water has a very calming effect and helps you overcome the panic you feel. Start using your brain (it's the best piece of survival equipment you possess) to puzzle out what has happened and, more importantly, what you are going to do next. Find a log to sit down on and stay there for at least thirty minutes. This will give you time to work through the feelings of panic you experience and overcome the urge to keep moving in hopes of finding your way out. After thirty minutes, the adrenaline that flooded through your system will have subsided and you can now objectively evaluate your situation, determine what needs to be done, and then put your plan into action.

Don't let the promises you have made to others override your need to protect yourself. Often these promises, as in *"Honey, I'll be home for dinner at seven"* or *"Boss, I'll be at work in the morning"* can cause survivors to continue trying to find their way out when they should be thinking about a fire, shelter, and staying put for the night. **Break that promise and protect yourself!**

As with most things *"It is a lot easier to prevent horrific things from happening than it is to correct the problem after it has occurred!"* This is certainly true in the case of "Staying Found." Those who recreate in the outdoors should become proficient in the use of a map and a compass. A GPS receiver is also a very useful navigation aid.

While it is not possible to learn to use a map, compass, and GPS receiver in the next few lines, the following tips might help you become a more proficient navigator:

- Buy an orienteering compass that can be adjusted for local declination.
- With an engraving pencil or other sharp point engrave the color of the north pointing end of the compass needle on the back of the compass base plate, i.e. R = N (red equals north). In a panic, it's easy to forget which end points north.
- Avoid using your compass around metallic objects which will deflect the needle and give you a false reading.
- Keep your GPS receiver away from your compass. There have been reports of the electronic fields surrounding the receiver affecting the magnetic orientation of the compass needle.
- Carry two compasses – if they both indicate the same direction to camp, then proceed in the direction indicated. When you are in trouble, it's easy to believe one compass is defective when it doesn't point in the "right" direction!
- Learn how to walk a straight line heading using your compass It may not be the most efficient method to get from one point to another, but it is the most reliable.

- Always mark your starting point on your map before you depart.
- ***When using a GPS receiver, ALWAYS mark your departure point.*** Unless the device knows where "home" is, it won't be able to take you there later. Always check your way point list and make sure "home" is recorded.

Out After Dark
– *coping with nyctophobia!*

What, you may ask, is nyctophobia? Simply put, it is "an exaggerated and unreasonable fear of the darkness." You may then ask what does nyctophobia have to do with you surviving an emergency. The short answer is that more people than you might imagine are "scared of the dark" or, more accurately, that they are afraid of what they can't see because it is dark! These people, when precipitated into an emergency and finding they have to spend an unplanned night out, can become incapacitated by their fear. They panic and do things that make a bad situation even worse!

During the daylight hours, the greatest part of our sensory input is derived from what we see. At night, especially during moonless periods, we can see very little and depend more on our ears to tell us what is going on around us and, since we haven't spent much time out in the dark, the origins of the sounds we hear are unknown to us. We fear what we don't understand! Our mind begins to make mountains out of molehills - the smallest of sounds becomes the greatest of terrors!

In part, our fear of the dark results from our parent's effort to keep us safe when we were young. Many of us grew up in what I call a "night-light" home. Parents, concerned about our safety, placed "night-lights" in strategic locations around the house so that we could to get a drink of water or visit the bathroom without bumping into the furniture or falling down the stairs! This well-intentioned concern for our safety resulted in young people, now adults, who have never been in the dark! Over time we have also been conditioned by our daily routines. The sun comes up and we are active. The sun sets and it's time to go to bed. We are generally indoors and sleeping during the hours of darkness! Additionally, many of us have come to believe in Murphy and his laws, one of which states: *"If it's going to go wrong, it's going to go wrong at night!"*

The hours of darkness, even for those who are not intimidated by darkness, create an environment that is new and different. Or, perhaps it's not so different! When you stop and think about it, nothing has changed. The rocks are still in the same place! The trees haven't moved! The slope of the land remains the same! You can still feel the grass beneath your feet! Perhaps the only thing that is different is the presence of the nocturnal fauna – insects, bats, a small number of reptiles, some birds, and a few other animals. Herein lays the problem! Our fear is a result of our inability to identify what we are hearing and our awareness that there is "something out there" that we can't see that might cause us harm! The cricket chirping under a nearby leaf becomes a mountain lion about to have us for dinner!

As a consequence of all this, people panic or, to put it more accurately, they experience "panic disorder" defined as " *sudden and often unexpected feelings of intense apprehension and impending doom coupled with typical physiological sensations (cardiovascular, respiratory, feelings such as of choking and smothering, nausea, sweating and trembling, dizziness).*"

So, what do you do about your nyctophobia? You can't change how you were brought up, but you can identify your fears and phobias. Gradual "exposure" is one way to allay your fears. The first step could be to spend time in your backyard at night listening to the dogs bark, the fire engine sirens and the other night sounds that you are familiar with. From there, visit the local city park or a nearby rural area where you are more likely to hear unfamiliar "wild" sounds. Go with someone both for personal security reasons and, if you choose your companion carefully, that person may be able to identify the yodel of a coyote, the calls of night birds or the chirping of a cricket! A camping trip is another opportunity to increase your exposure to darkness and, in turn, your comfort level. Take a chair, move away from the campfire, turn out all the lights (lanterns, flashlights, etc.) and sit back and enjoy the evening. Over time, you will come to realize that the night is no more dangerous than any other time of the day – it's just different. It's dark!

When faced with a night out, take the time to look around before it gets too dark and orient yourself in relation to the nearby trees, rocks, shape of the land, etc. Doing so will enable you to identify the many shadows that will appear after the sun sets and help to alleviate any fears that might develop with the appearance of various shapes in the darkness. Even on the darkest night, once your eyes become accustomed to the available light, it will surprise you how much you can see - especially if you use your peripheral vision! Rather than looking at an object directly, look slightly off to one side and it will appear much clearer to you. On a clear, star-filled night, the silhouette of the surrounding landscape can be seen which will help to keep you oriented should you decide to travel. (Not usually advisable!) On bright moonlit nights, the amount of light available may once again surprise you and, under these conditions, moving around is very possible.

Try not to use a flashlight. The beam of light extending out from a flashlight limits your vision to only that area illuminated by the shaft of light. Using a flashlight also affects your night vision. It will be more difficult to see in the dark until sufficient time has elapsed after the light has been extinguished to allow the pupils in your eye to dilate and for your night vision to return. Save the flashlight for when you have to move and you are confronted with rough terrain where each foot needs to be placed carefully to avoid an accident.

Survivors may find that they will be more active at night when it is too cold to sleep comfortably and less active during the day when the warmer conditions allow sleep. Being able to function safely at night will depend on understanding the impact of reduced visibility and, at the same time, knowing that the environment is not inherently more dangerous just because of the darkness. What previously would have been a terror-filled night-without-end can now become an enjoyable new experience!

Becoming Stranded

The very word ***"stranded"*** brings to mind the story of Robinson Crusoe's lengthy stay on his tropical island or the plight of the Donner Party. The experiences of the Uruguayan rugby team who survived a crash landing in the Andes as told in Piers Paul Read's book "Alive" also comes to mind. If the truth be told, you can become stranded in far less exotic places than the South Pacific, the Andes or the Sierra Madre Mountains of California. If the truth be told you can become stranded and find yourself having to survive in the woodlot behind your home. You can become stranded when driving to work or as a result of many other scenarios where suddenly you are unable to continue or to return to safety. Weather, mechanical breakdown, the onset of darkness, or other accidents can all result in your having to utilize survival skills and procedures to insure that you see the light of the next day. It happens all the time. Take for instance the case of Karen Webster of Nelson, South Dakota, who left work one winter morning after working the night shift to drive home only to find herself a few minutes later stuck in a snowdrift on an isolated country lane unable to proceed. Some forty-four hours later, she was finally found and rescued. Her advice to others: *"It can happen to anyone. Make sure you're equipped. Stay with your vehicle. Tell someone where you're going!"* Karen survived becoming stranded because she followed her own advice, she was prepared and she believed she would be rescued. She didn't panic – she survived!

Unless you have experienced the emotions of finding yourself stranded a long way from help it is difficult to explain in words the gut wrenching fear you feel when all of a sudden you realize you can't get back, you're cut-off, you're alone without anyone to help – **YOU MIGHT DIE!**

- ***Mechanical Failure***

  Unfortunately most people have an unfounded faith in their vehicles' ability to perform forever! It should be a given that if man made it, it can and will break down! Knowing this, steps should be taken to be able to fix the problem or, at the very least, you should be able to contact others for help in the event you become stranded. When traveling to places where help is a long way off, prepare your vehicle accordingly. Often the malfunction is not something catastrophic. It's usually the failure of some part that, had the operator performed a simple visual check, the situation could have been prevented. Simple steps like checking the fluid levels – all fluid levels, not just the oil - checking air pressure in the tires, and checking the condition of belts and hoses are often all that is necessary to complete an uneventful trip. While it may not be possible to eliminate all mechanical failures, it is possible to minimize the likelihood of becoming stranded because of mechanical malfunction by **thoroughly inspecting your vehicle before a trip and equipping it with sufficient emergency gear to keep the occupants safe until found.**

- ***Miscommunication***

  As the pilot flew back to Fairbanks after dropping my sheep hunting partner and me off, I was left with some misgivings regarding his understanding of when we were to be picked up. My misgivings became reality ten days later when our ride home failed to show up. While I was waiting for the overdue transportation, some troubling thoughts came to me. Such as: *"I wonder if the plane that dropped us off crashed on its way back to base." "I wonder if the pilot told anyone else where he had taken us." "I wonder if anyone will come looking for us!"*

Several days passed before we finally heard the drone of the Super Cub, our ride home, coming across the tundra. In this instance, it was confusion between "picking us up ten days later" and "picking us up on the 10th" that led to the miscommunication. Had we not planned on "weather days" and a delayed pickup, our hunting trip might have become a survival experience. **Critical communications should be written down, not verbally communicated! Plan for delays.**

- ***Darkness***

Suffice it to say that, once the sun sets, a person can be just as stranded as they are when their car breaks down miles from sources of assistance. Traveling on foot at night is not generally recommended. Stay put and wait for the sun to come up and then decide what should be done.

- ***Accidents***

The problem with modern transportation is that, in a very short period of time, you can find yourself a long way from help after an accident. In a couple of hours, an ATV traveling at 12 mph can put you 24 miles from the trail head. How long will it take you to walk 24 miles? You can find yourself many miles from the marina when the boat that you were speeding across the lake in col-

> lides with a semi-sunken log and sinks. How far can you swim? A light aircraft flying at 100 mph places you even further back in the wilderness – usually too far to walk out. Regardless of the mode of transportation, you are now a long way from home – you are stranded and must survive until rescue arrives. **Will you be able to survive until you are found and rescued?**

Suffering Illness or Injury

Both illness and injury have resulted in people finding themselves unable to continue their trips into the backcountry and, more importantly, being unable to make it back to medical care – they had to be rescued. It is more common for incapacitating injuries to occur than it is for a person to become so ill that they have to be rescued. The value of having completed a comprehensive wilderness medical program cannot be overemphasized, especially when you are faced with treating a companion who has suffered life threatening injuries. Incapacitating illness in the backcountry can be much more difficult to deal with since the average person is not trained to first diagnose the problem and then treat it. The lack of the appropriate medications makes the problem even more difficult. In this situation the best that can be done is to make the victim as comfortable as possible and then go for help.

Weather

Most commonly it is the onset of inclement weather that results in people having to survive. Motorists are stranded in their cars on the highways when driving conditions become too dangerous to continue – or, more commonly, they continue driving until an accident happens. Those recreating outdoors suddenly find themselves unable to return home because the snow gets too deep, the water in the river rises and crossing becomes too risky, or fog obscures the landmarks and navigation becomes impossible.

Becoming stranded is not the end of the world! If you have told others of your travel plans, they will become worried when you don't show up and will initiate the rescue process by contacting the authorities. **As the one who is stranded, your job is to keep yourself alive until they show up**.

6

Staying Found Is Better Than Being Lost!

"All outdoor users should carry and know how to use a map and compass before they go off into the backcountry."

The first step in staying found is locating your position and marking that position on your map before you leave your vehicle or camp. Then identify the boundaries that surround the area in which you will be traveling. These boundaries could be prominent roads, railways, power lines or large rivers. Preferably, you should identify boundaries on all four sides of the area you will be in. Mark these boundaries with a yellow or green highlighter pen. Having located yourself on the map and knowing the boundaries, you can then leave camp with the knowledge that, if you get lost, all you have to do is determine which boundary is closest (this may be an educated guess) and walk a straight line to it. Having located yourself, make

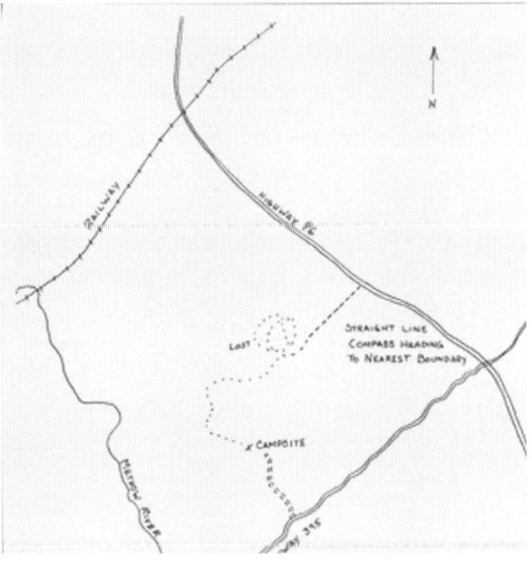

your way to your original starting point. It can be a long walk back, but at least you will know where you are! In some situations less than four boundaries may be clearly identifiable and, if this is the case, determine which direction you would have to travel to get back to the boundary you started from. If you walked north away from a road you would have to follow a southerly heading to return to the road.

Many people experience great difficulty walking a straight line and have wandered in circles until exhausted. The simplest way to walk a straight line is to use a compass, preferably an "orienteering compass." Having determined the direction to the nearest boundary, point the "direction of travel arrow" towards your destination then turn the dial of the compass until "N" coincides with the north end of the compass needle. Follow the direction indicated by the direction-of-travel arrow always keeping the north end of the compass needle and the orienteering arrow aligned. Look up, sight on a landmark, and walk to it. Repeat these steps until you reach the boundary and can relocate yourself. In some areas, only one significant boundary may be present. In this situation, determine before you leave camp the direction you will have to travel to get to the boundary in the event you become disoriented.

Often the road or trail leading to your camp will serve as a primary boundary. If you walk in a westerly direction away from your camp, you will have to walk directly opposite that, or easterly, to return to the road or trail where your camp is located.

Any metal object that is nearby may radically affect the compass needle - do not let firearms, knives, large metal belt buckles or other compasses near your compass when taking a reading or following a compass heading.

The cardinal directions, north, east, south and west, can be determined without a compass using the following procedures. Using a watch with hands, point the hour hand directly at the sun. The point half way between the hour hand and 12 o'clock will point generally SOUTH. North will be directly opposite. At night, a line drawn through the two "pointer stars" in the bowl of the Big Dipper and extended approximately four times the distance between the two stars intersects Polaris, the North Star, which is never more than one degree from True North. Lay a stick on the ground aligned with north so that you can determine the cardinal directions the following morning.

Everybody should carry and know how to use a map. Many kinds of maps are available and can be obtained from county, state, or provincial agencies, the US Forest Service, and other sources. The most useful maps, called topographic maps, may be purchased at many sporting goods outlets, some book stores, or ordered directly from the US Geological Service. Topographic maps show both man-made features (drawn in black or red) and natural features (drawn in green for vegetation and blue for water). Contour lines, lines drawn on a map joining points of equal elevation above sea level, are drawn in brown and show the altitude and the terrain features of the land mass covered by the map.

You will find other useful information in the marginal information of the map. The scale enables the user to measure the distance between two points on the map. The declination diagram shows the difference between True and Magnetic North. The date the map was printed - remember changes take place over time that may not be reflected on the map. Map symbols enable the user to interpret the information shown. Remember, unless shown otherwise, north is always at the top of the map.

The basic information presented here is designed to enable outdoor users to relocate themselves after becoming disoriented and to make their way back to safety. Orienteering clubs, mountaineering equipment shops and other recreation programs offer additional wilderness navigation training that you can take to refine your navigation skills and increase your confidence to travel the back country without getting lost.

LOST... NOW WHAT

OK so you're lost and the day is coming to an end. You are faced with a night out that you hadn't planned on. However because you had considered the possibility of such an event occurring, it's not totally unexpected. You have your survival kit, an extra sweater and a rain suit to keep you warm. You have managed to overcome the initial urge to keep moving and now it's time to settle in for the night. Look for the most protected area you can find, an area out of the wind - it's easier to cope with ambient air temperature than it is wind chill. Look for a level area under the protection offered by the limbs of a large tree. Move uphill out of cold air sinks. Look around for any naturally occurring shelter – caves, overhangs, etc.

Add layers of clothing before you get cold. Locate any available firewood and build a fire. You will find that a fire is a valuable companion in addition to all the other benefits it provides the survivor. Once a fire is burning and you are sheltered, you are "home." With the camp chores done, your thoughts will turn again to those you are separated from – your buddies in camp or perhaps family members at home who are expecting you for dinner. Here, the need to be reunited with them will emerge and you will be tempted to keep moving. RESIST THE TEMPTATION! Traveling at night in unfamiliar country is dangerous.

It is possible that, as the sky darkens, you will be able to see the lights of distant homes or towns and, again, be tempted to make your way towards them. Survivors tend to underestimate distance and overestimate their ability to travel to a distant destination. Sit tight. Survive. Be alive when the sun comes up in the morning! Crawl into your plastic bag shelter or under a lean-to made from a blue-crinkly tarp and get some sleep. Depending on the temperature you will probably wake up frequently during the night as your body cools. Exercise. Eat some food. Have a drink and then go back to sleep again. In cold conditions it may be necessary to be more active during the night to keep yourself warm. Don't get spooked by the night sounds. Our minds tend to make mountains-out-of-molehills. Take heart, the sun will come up the next morning; the weather will improve, you will "find" yourself once again and make your way back to worried, but now relieved, family and friends.

S – Stop moving around
T – Think about what needs to be done
O – Observe your surroundings
P – Plan a course of action and implement it

Becoming lost is serious but it does not have to be dangerous if you react properly. An acronym to help you remember what to do is STOP. Sit down and don't panic. Talk positively to yourself - out loud! Have a drink of water or eat a candy bar. Remember your brain is the best piece of survival equipment you have -- use it. Think about your situation. How bad is it really? Are there injuries that you need to tend to? Are you loosing body heat? What needs to be done first? How much time do you have before it gets dark or before the storm breaks? Observe the area. What resources are available to help you survive? What natural hazards exist? Plan what to do next -- but be flexible. Remember, you have no control over the weather or the onset of darkness, but you do have control over your actions!

When you become lost, the first thing you must do is admit to yourself that you don't know where you are -- you're lost! Or more ac curately, you don't know how to get back to your starting point. While you are sitting, go over in your mind what you did since leaving your car or camp earlier in the day and compare your recollections with the information provided by your map. What landmarks did you see along the way? Can you see these landmarks on your map? Have you been going uphill or down? How many rivers did you cross? How many ridges did you climb? Did you leave tracks that you can follow back to your starting point? It helps to draw a map in the ground. By a process of deduction, you may be able to unscramble your thoughts and reorient yourself. Often you'll find that you're not as lost as you first thought you were!

Unless you can positively locate yourself, the best advice to follow is to stay put and not travel. Do not run around looking for something familiar. Not only will this further confuse you, it will exhaust you, dehydrate you, and increase the likelihood of injuring yourself. It will also make the searcher's job much more difficult. You may move into an area that has already been searched and may not be searched again until all other possibilities have been investigated! Wait for the rescuers to find you. They are trained and equipped to rescue the lost and injured. Sit tight, protect yourself, signal and let them find you. Remember that most rescues in the United States are accomplished within 72 hours, especially if you have told someone where you were going! Your job is to survive until they arrive.

7

Survival Medicine

"Survival becomes impossible when the body's defenses can no longer match the insults of the environment."

As I have analyzed the stories of survivors and the survival situations they found themselves in I have come to the conclusion that there are two underlying causes for the medical difficulties the survivors experienced. First there appears to be a lack of understanding of the impact of the environment on human physiology. Secondly, survivors, lacking specific survival training, appropriate clothing and survival equipment, are left to cope with the situation as best they can relying on their "will-to-survive, their ability to improvise and luck!" Not a good situation. This chapter will look at some of the physiological threats to the body and suggest ways to minimize the impact of the threats.

Within the context of a wilderness emergency, disabling illnesses include hypothermia, dehydration, illnesses associated with going to high altitude (8,000 feet and above) too quickly, and any other malady that limits a person's ability to survive. These same illnesses can result in a person becoming incapacitated to the point where they are unable to help themselves and only outside intervention will prevent a tragedy from occurring. From a physiological point of view, surviving a wilderness emergency is a process of keeping everything in balance. To avoid hypothermia (dangerously low body temperature) or hyperthermia (dangerously high body temperature), we must achieve thermal balance; to avoid dehydration, we must achieve water balance; and to avoid starvation, we must obtain food. Of these, maintaining thermal balance and preventing dehydration are the most important concerns to the survivor.

Maintaining Thermal Balance – *preventing hypothermia and hyperthermia*

In a cold environment, where the human body is warmer than the environment, heat will be lost to the surroundings. In a hot environment, where the human body may be cooler than the environment, heat can be gained from the surroundings. Either situation can be life-threatening.

In a cold environment, the heat lost from the body through the processes of radiation, convection, conduction, and evaporation must be balanced by metabolism, i.e., the heat produced within each of the body's cells. When there is insufficient energy to produce this heat, we experience hypothermia which can quickly impair our ability to function – mentally and physically. Maintaining thermal balance in cold weather requires sufficient intake of food to produce approximately 3,500 calories of heat per day. Lacking food, the foods stored in the body in the form of fat, carbohydrates, and protein become the primary source of energy and, since this is a finite amount, it becomes increasingly more difficult to function as these supplies are depleted. Maintaining thermal balance also requires the use of appropriate clothing to retain the heat that the body is producing within the fabric and between the layers of clothing and, in so doing, keep us warm. When there is insufficient clothing, heat lost by radiation, evaporation, convection, and conduction can quickly exceed body heat production and hypothermia will result.

In a hot environment, thermal balance is achieved by continually cooling the body and minimizing thermal gain from the surroundings. Heat loss by evaporation is the body's primary way of dumping heat, but this is only effective where there is sufficient water within the body to be evaporated. Heat gain from the surroundings can be reduced by seeking shade and by minimizing contact with objects that are hotter than the body. The lack of water and shade can quickly cause the survivor's body temperature to rise to the point where mental and physical function is impaired and survival for any prolonged period of time becomes questionable.

Maintaining Water Balance – *preventing dehydration*

Under normal circumstances, a person's minimum water losses each day (urination, defecation, and the water needed to humidify the air we breath) will be around 1.5 quarts. Some of this water will be replaced by the water produced by metabolism. The rest, about one quart, must be consumed to maintain water balance. When available, survivors should drink three to four quarts of water per day to replace the water lost during the process of surviving, i.e., gathering firewood, building shelters, moving, etc. Because of circumstance, it is entirely possible that a survivor may not be able to obtain the recommended amounts of water each day and, consequently, will find himself in a "water deficit" situation very quickly. Some will even begin their survival episode already dehydrated!

There are too many variables to be able to accurately predict how long a person will live with reduced quantities of water. A better survival strategy would be to develop methods of gathering and using any available water and practicing intelligent water conservation procedures that make the best possible use of the available water. Where the availability of water is limited, survivors should not drink any water for the first 24 hours – the body's reserves should be able to cope in the early stages of a survival experience. After the first day, stringent rationing of available water can quickly lead to impaired judgment and physical performance. *"Ration your sweat not your water."* Dehydration quickly reduces your ability to function effectively and safely. Drink the water! The only water that will help you is the water in your stomach. The water in your canteen is doing you no good!

In North America, lacking the means to purify water, it is better to drink from any available water source, even though it may contain harmful organisms, and prevent dehydration than not to drink the water and suffer the more immediate effects of dehydration. *"Doctors can cure giardia, but they can't fix dead!*

Maintaining Food Balance

The requirement for food is subordinate to the need to maintain body temperature and the need for water. Many have survived for long periods of time without any food living entirely off of the "food" stored in their bodies in the form of fat, carbohydrates, and protein. Despite this, lack of food is still a threat to your survival. As each day passes without food or with only limited food, your ability to function is increasingly impaired – you won't have the energy to do what needs to be done. Your ability to keep warm will be reduced. Since the sources of energy are limited, all activities should be carefully considered by the survivor in terms of the energy expended. The survivor has to balance the energy expended while procuring food from the land against the energy derived from the food. It usually is best to save your energy!

Injury

Surviving necessitates being able to deal with any injuries that occur. People are injured in many ways, but, most commonly, serious injuries occur when they are involved in a vehicle accident or when *"they fall off mountains or mountains fall on them."* Few people begin their survival experience uninjured. The survival books and the "how-to-survive" articles written in the popular outdoor press don't talk about how the injured survivor is to build a shelter, start fires and do all the other tasks needed to live to tell the tale. They make the assumption that the reader will be fully functional and capable of accomplishing the tasks they describe in the text. Most often, this is not the case!

Disabling injuries, such as fractures of the lower extremities, injuries to the spine and head, and eye damage usually rule out the possibility of making it back without outside help. Serious burns covering large portions of the body also make moving around very difficult, if not impossible. Significant blood losses resulting from the trauma following falls or vehicle accidents, once again, severely limit a person's ability to function. Survival begins with being able to cope with the injuries sustained in the accident and then satisfying the other basic survival needs – protection, hydration, warmth, etc. If you can't stop the blood squirting out of your arm, the need for shelters, fire and signaling are immaterial!

When was the last time you attended a Red Cross First Aid Course? Could you perform CPR on your spouse or a child should the need arise? Have you considered taking a Wilderness First Responder course? Do your traveling companions have any emergency medical skills in the event that you are the one that needs help? Do you carry a first aid kit? Do you know how to use the contents of the kit? Your answers to these questions could have life-saving implications! If your knowledge and skills are deficient, then remedy this problem first before going on to developing your field survival skills.

Assemble a good medical kit. It is not necessary to be able to deal with every medical eventuality. Rather, gather the equipment and medications that can be used to treat the injuries and ailments more commonly experienced by people recreating or working in the outdoors. One piece of medical equipment that I would not be without is a SAM® SPLINT. This inexpensive device, when combined with an elastic bandage, makes stabilizing a severe sprain, strain or fracture much easier. Another very practical, inexpensive tool to include in your medical kit is a pair of Emergency Medical Technician shears. You will find many uses for them.

More advanced backcountry medical training can be obtained from many providers. Attending one of the many wilderness medicine conferences that are held around the country is a very good way to improve both your medical knowledge and skills. *See* Appendix on page 139, for training programs that provide wilderness Continuing Medical Education (CME), Wilderness First Aid, Wilderness First Responder and Wilderness Emergency Medical Technician training.

8

Weather

"You can't govern the elements but you can govern your actions."

Statistics in this chapter are courtesy of NOAA

Why is it so many people come to grief each year in weather-related accidents? Why is it, with all of the weather information we have available to us, people still find themselves trapped by storms, isolated by blizzards, caught out away from home or base camp by weather conditions that endanger their lives? I believe part of the problem lies in our arrogance. Our belief that "we can handle it" whatever "it" happens to be. Many have an unwavering belief in their ability to overcome the difficulties that wind, rain, plummeting temperatures, scalding heat and other extremes that weather may bring – some of these people die! When you look back over the past thirty years in the United States, each year approximately 71 people are killed by lightning; 219 people die from heat-related illnesses; 27 succumb to the cold; and tornadoes kill 65 people. Each year, floods drown 127 people and 1,800 more are thought to die in cold water incidents across the country. A further 52 die in winter storms. Hurricanes result in 16 more deaths.

The numbers shown are the fatalities – many more people suffered from the impact of the weather.

In the grand scheme of things, these are not large numbers when compared to the numbers of non-weather related death across the country. However, would you want to be one of the ones that died? Of course not! So what can be done to insure that you don't become one of the unfortunate statistics? Let's take a closer look at these weather problems and see what can be done to reduce the impact of weather on the activities that take us into the outdoors and on our safety.

LIGHTNING

Lightning is probably the least understood threat to your safety of all of the weather-related hazards. Of the three hundred or so people each year that are hit by lightning, one third die and a high percentage of the remainder will suffer long-term, often life-long, medical difficulties. While some who are killed and injured are inside, the vast majority are either working or recreating outside.

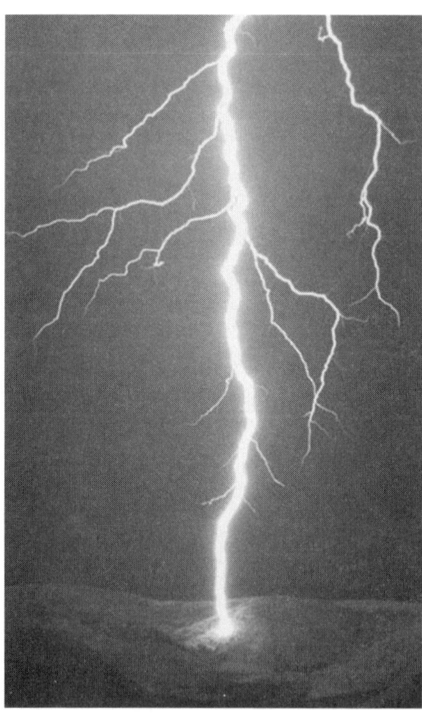

Safety Rules

1. Keep an eye on the sky. Pay attention to developing storms - increasing wind speeds, anvil shaped clouds with lightning are all signs of an approaching storm.
2. Be proactive – don't wait until you are getting wet to suspend your outdoor activities. Move into a substantial building or an enclosed vehicle. A large dry cave also offers protection, but move away from the entrance – shallow

caves and rocky overhangs offer little or no protection. Move away from isolated, exposed high ground and move toward lower, less exposed areas. THERE ARE NO "SAFE" AREAS - JUST "SAFER" AREAS!

3. The sound of thunder is a warning that a storm is brewing. Thunder can be heard up to ten miles away. If you can hear thunder you are close enough to be hit! Take shelter now.
4. Don't be, or be connected to, the tallest object in the area. If caught outside, move into low trees of even height and stand away from the tree trunks. If above the tree line, crouch down in the lowest area you can find. Stay away from isolated trees. It is better to crouch down in the open than shelter under a tree that stands alone in a field.
5. Water is a great conductor of electricity – get out of water at the first sign of a storm developing. If in a boat, go directly to the shore and move into shelter. Continuing to swim, boat, wade or any other activity related to water is dangerous.
6. Move away from all metal that might conduct electricity (fences, railway lines, buildings, road barricades, and telephone lines) and remove all metal (jewelry, metal framed glasses, coins, etc.) from your body. Metal in contact with your skin can cause serious burns if you are hit.
7. If part of a group, spread out. Staying together increases the chance of more than one person being injured.
8. If you smell ozone, if your hair stands on end, or if you experience any other unusual phenomena, a lightning strike could be imminent – protect yourself.

HOT TEMPERATURES

Heat causes more deaths each year than any other category of weather related fatalities and, of these deaths, most occur in urban areas and in cities during heat waves. The young and the old are most at risk. Those who die from heat related illness in the outdoors are people who become stranded as a result of vehicle accidents and those who become lost or other circumstances that trap them in hot, arid regions without sufficient water to maintain life. Excessive heat also increases the risk of dying from other causes.

Safety Rules

1. As ambient temperature rises, your body's need for water will increase. The evaporation of water from the skin is the body's primary way of eliminating excess heat. Without water to sweat, body temperature will continue to rise until cell function ceases and you die.

Desert Shelter

2. When the environment is hotter than 98.6° F you will gain heat from the environment and your body temperature will rise. Finding shade and adequate supplies of water are critical to your survival.
3. Be especially careful in hot, humid environments where the high humidity interferes with your body's ability to sweat efficiently. Water that is dripping from your skin does not remove heat.

4. Salt is important to your well being, but it is not necessary to take salt tablets. The salt you eat with your meals is sufficient. During periods of severe heat, eating saltier foods (pretzels, potato chips, etc.) will help to replace the salts lost in sweating. Drinking large quantities of water and not consuming enough salt can result in hyponatremia - a medical condition that can be fatal.

COLD TEMPERATURES

Man is a tropical animal and has to rely on clothing, shelter and food to maintain a body temperature of 98.6° F! Exposure to temperatures below normal body temperature without adequate protection will eventually result in hypothermia which can become life threatening if not reversed quickly. A lowering of your body temperatures quickly starts a chain of events that begins with shivering, reduced hand and finger dexterity, and ends with cardiac arrest.

Safety rules

1. Wear, or have with you, clothing that will keep you warm and dry when weather conditions place your safety at risk.
2. Wear, or have with you, clothing that prevents wind from penetrating your clothing.
3. Put on additional clothing before you become chilled.
4. Your head must receive special attention. Carry a stocking cap and a windproof hood to put on when temperatures drop and wind speed increases.
5. Temperatures do not have to be extreme to quickly loose hand and finger dexterity. Gloves and mittens should be a part of your emergency clothing.
6. Select footwear that will keep your feet warm and dry.

WIND

Wind is an insidious threat to your safety. Unlike finding yourself in an extreme cold or hot environment where the danger is more obvious, wind is generally thought of as an annoying phenomenon without significant life threatening ramifications until tornadoes and hurricanes enter the picture. What we forget is that, as long as wind is moving across the surface of exposed skin, heat is being removed. In hot conditions this can be beneficial; however, in cold conditions, this heat loss and the subsequent drop in body temperature can become life threatening. An outer layer of clothing that is not only waterproof but also windproof is a vital part of your clothing ensemble. Studies have shown that with a windproof outer layer, you can get by with much less insulation.

The combined effect of wind and temperature, wind-chill, creates a condition where the temperature itself isn't that low, but to know how cold it feels, you have to figure in the effect of the wind. The "wind-chill" charts used by weather forecasters have recently been revised and now more accurately portray the danger faced by people when recreating in windy cold conditions.

Safety rules

1. Carry a windproof, waterproof outer layer and put it on before you get cold.
2. In windy situations, turn your back to the wind and then look for any obstruction or barrier that you can find shelter behind. Once out of the wind, you only need to protect yourself from the ambient temperature, not the wind-chill - the difference can be life-saving!

FLASH FLOODS

Most flash flooding is caused by slow-moving thunderstorms repeatedly moving over the same area or heavy rains from hurricanes and tropical storms. The two key elements that contribute to flash flooding are rainfall intensity and duration. Intensity is the rate of rainfall and duration is how long the rain lasts. Topography, soil conditions, and ground cover also play an important role. Flash floods can occur within a few minutes or may occur within hours of heavy rainfall. Rapidly rising water can reach heights of thirty feet or more and can trigger catastrophic mudslides.

Safety rules

1. Pay attention to the warnings and watches announced by the National Weather Service and your local radio. You will not always have a warning that these deadly, sudden floods are coming. Many deaths occur because the victims waited too long to take action or were distracted while trying to save personal belongings.
2. NEVER try to walk, swim or drive through swift water. If you come upon flood waters, STOP! TURN AROUND AND GO ANOTHER WAY. Even six inches of fast-moving water can knock you off your feet and water two feet deep will float your car!
3. PLAN AHEAD. Determine ahead of time where you would go if you were told to evacuate. Select higher ground where you could climb above the high water. Many flash floods occur at night greatly complicating evacuation efforts.
4. The sound of distant thunder could forewarn you of the possibility of flooding.
5. Watch for quickly rising water and if present take action quickly.

Stay informed about the weather by listening to NOAA weather radio, commercial radio, and television for the latest watches, warnings, and advisories. Plan your activities around the forecasted weather. Decide what you will do when the weather deteriorates and implement the plan **BEFORE** you are in danger. Weather can make you very uncomfortable, but you don't have to die because of it.

A *weather radio is the best means to receive warnings from the* National Weather Service which continuously broadcasts updated weather warnings and forecasts. Depending on topography, the average range for these radios is about 40 miles. Purchase a radio that has both a battery backup and a tone-alert feature which automatically alerts you when a watch or warning is issued.

It is often weather that causes an aircraft to crash-land or ditch – particularly light aircraft and helicopters! It is the weather, or more accurately, the lack of awareness of how quickly that the weather can change, that precipitates a person into a survival situation! One moment the sun is out and hiking in shorts and a T-shirt is appropriate. Moments later, the sun goes behind a cloud, it begins to rain, the wind velocity increases a few miles per hour, the temperature plummets, and now the victim is in a situation from which he may not recover. Never assume anything. As Left Kreh, the well known author and fly fisherman once said *"It's always going to be colder than they tell you. It's going to be windier than it should be for the time of year and it's going to rain more than you expect it to so be prepared for anything."*

9

Selecting Cold Weather Clothing

"There's no such thing as bad weather, just bad clothing."

So there you are! It has finally happened! You're lost. The sun is setting and it looks like there's a storm brewing. As much as you would like to be back in camp, the realization slowly sets in that you're going to have to spend a night out that you hadn't planned on. Despite your acceptance of the situation, you still feel very ill-at-ease. This isn't going to be comfortable. You can already feel the temperature dropping and the wind is picking up. So what to do first? Get a fire going? Find a shelter? Try and signal your buddies back in camp? Wait a minute! Let's go back to basics: You are not going to be in any better shape than you are at this moment. You're warm, reasonably hydrated, uninjured, and haven't panicked yet. Let's keep it that way!

Your warmth during the night will largely be determined by the clothing you are wearing and its ability to retain the heat your body is producing. Your clothing may turn out to be the only shelter you can count on and your body heat may be the only heat available to you. Circumstances often preclude building the kinds of shelters shown in survival articles and books. Your circumstances may also preclude your ability to build and maintain a fire! Since this is the case, careful attention should be paid to selecting clothing that will protect you in an emergency.

"You should dress to survive, not just to arrive!"

When selecting clothing, always consider the possibility that you may have to spend a night out in it and ask the question, "Will it keep me warm when I'm sitting still?" It may not be practical to wear all of the clothing you need for that night out, so carry with you additional insulating layers and a windproof, waterproof garment to use when the time comes to sit out a storm, while waiting for the sun to rise, or for rescue to arrive.

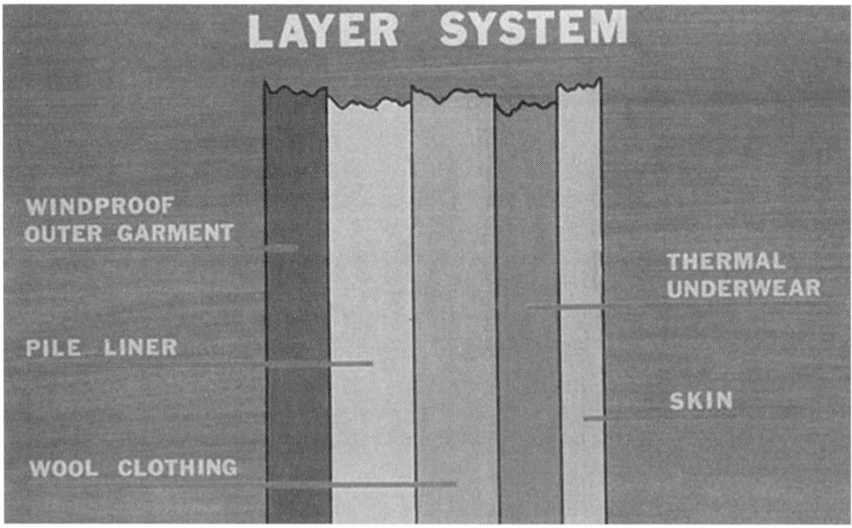

When selecting clothing for use in the outdoors, *think* "system." A clothing system should create a micro climate around the body that protects the wearer from wind and cold temperatures and enables the wearer to function efficiently and safely. The system should include three layers: the skin layer which provides some insulation, but, more importantly, moves water away from the skin; the inner layers which insulate; and the outer layer which prevents water and wind penetration. Each layer is important. This system allows the wearer to acclimate easily to the climate by removing layers when the body is heating up and sweat vapor is becoming water droplets, and by replacing layers when temperatures fall or activity levels decrease and the body begins to cool.

"The first rule of staying warm is to stay dry and keep the wind out."

In all of its forms, water is your enemy! Whether you become wet from inside out because of the sweat you're producing or from the outside in because of rain or snow, the result is the same – compromised insulation and loss of body heat.

SKIN LAYERS

The human body is constantly giving off moisture through the skin in the form of insensible perspiration or sweat vapor. When your body temperature raises as a result of strenuous activity or increases in environmental temperature, sweating begins which results in sweat vapor changing to water droplets forming on the skin. This moisture will quickly saturate the layer of clothing next to the skin and, in turn, each successive layer unless body temperature decreases and sweating stops. When cotton is worn as the inner layer, it quickly absorbs the sweat and collapses offering no protection at all. In fact, it creates a dangerous situation where heat is conducted away from your body.

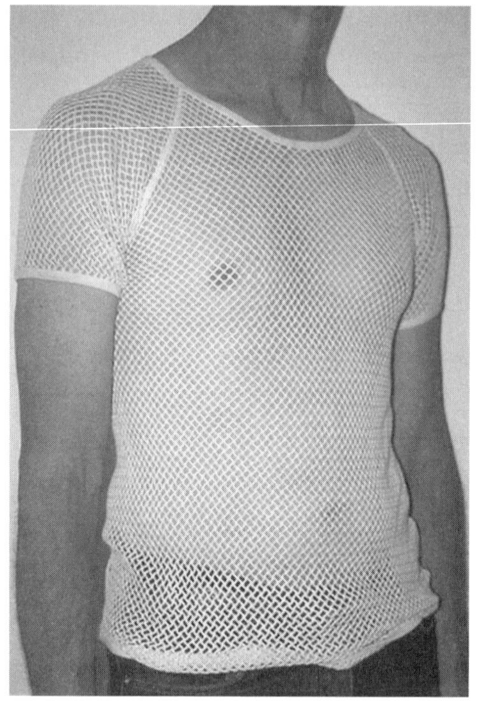

Synthetic fabrics, unlike cotton, absorb virtually no water and many are hydrophobic – they facilitate the movement of water from the warm, moist environment next to your skin towards the cooler, drier outer layers and beyond. The availability of "hi-tech" wool has made it possible to manufacture very good wool thermal underwear that is non-allergenic and doesn't "itch."

Fishnet long underwear has fallen out of favor but remains a very effective form of thermal protection. Other underwear fabrics include silk. Silk however, because it is a natural fiber, tends to absorb and hold water. It is also not as durable as the synthetic fabrics.

"To stay warm, stay cool! Don't sweat!"

THE INNER LAYERS

Depending on your level of activity, the number of inner layers worn will vary as environmental temperatures change. Despite the availability of a wide variety of technologically-advanced fabrics, it is still hard to beat wool for keeping yourself warm and for its durability under tough conditions – especially around fire! Wool, like the synthetics used for thermal underwear, has the ability to move sweat vapor through a garment. Additionally, when saturated, it has the ability to hold up to 30% of its weight in water within the core of the fiber, thereby moving water away from your body. Body heat gradually moves this water to the outside of the fiber and the outer surfaces of the clothing where it eventually evaporates. Wool also traps air between the fibers which helps to provide insulation from cold conditions – even when wet! On the downside, however, wet wool is heavy and takes a long time to dry. Some wool garments are not very windproof and must be used in conjunction with a windproof outer layer in windy conditions.

Synthetics can also be used for the inner layers. Fleece garments, in their many forms, are commonly made from polyester which, like synthetic underwear, dries rapidly, and retains much of its loft (ability to retain its airspace) when wet. Fleece clothing is available that is durable, comfortable to wear, and very warm. Remember, fleece is "plastic" and, as such, it does not tolerate heat! Get too close to the fire and you may find your jacket melting! Fleece is also subject to wind penetration unless combined with a "wind-blocking layer" or used with a windproof outer layer.

A layer of wool and/or fleece may still not be enough insulation to keep you warm – another insulating layer may be necessary. Once again the choice is between natural insulators (down and wool) and the synthetics. Down is a very effective insulating material but only when it can be kept dry. Many synthetic insulators are currently available and new ones (or at least new "names") seem to show up every day. "Lamalite," an insulation material used in Wiggy's cold weather clothing and sleeping bags, is the best. It has all of the advantages of down – loft and compressibility - and none of the bad – it retains much of its loft even when damp.

THE OUTER LAYERS

Wind is a grossly-underestimated threat to personal survival. Wind penetrating through the outer layers of clothing causes heat loss and places the wearer at risk of becoming hypothermic. Lacking an effective outer layer, a 9 mph wind can decrease the effectiveness of your insulation by as much as 30%! A person can get by with fewer insulating layers if the outer layer is completely windproof. In a windy environment, if lacking a windproof layer, get behind a rock or log, get over the ridge, or stand behind a tree – anything to remove yourself from the effects of wind-chill. It is much easier to contend with the ambient air temperature than it is the effects of wind-chill. The difference can be life saving! Many varieties of both windproof/waterproof and windproof/waterproof-breathable fabrics are on the market. Variations in temperature, an individual's activity level, cost and other factors will ultimately determine which fabric a person selects. A totally waterproof outer layer, such as Guide Jacket and bibs by Helly Hansen®, works well when the production of sweat is managed by reducing your activity level and by venting out the humid air from around your body by opening zippers.

AREAS OF SPECIAL CONCERN

Hands

Protect your hands. Keep them warm. Once your hands cool and you can no longer touch finger to thumb, you have lost the ability to perform many of the tasks needed to survive. Remember that hand and foot warmth is dependent on keeping the rest of your body warm. Put another way – your extremities are going to be sacrificed in order to keep your body core warm. A pair of light leather gloves - goat skin work best - will protect your hands from everyday injuries such as burns, nicks, cuts, bruises, abrasions, and broken finger nails, etc. They will also help to keep your hands warm. When the temperature drops and greater protection is needed, a pair of synthetic mittens is advisable. Carry both gloves and mittens for hand protection in the outdoors. As an emergency backup, include chemical hand warmers in your gear. When you lose hand and finger dexterity, activate two packages and slide one into each mitten.

Head

Put on additional clothing before you become cold. Pay particular attention to protecting your head – a bare head will loose a lot of heat. Cover it up even if you have to improvise a hat from other clothing items. One very useful head covering is a Head Sokz™. This waterproof, windproof head covering can be used in a variety of ways to effectively protect your head and neck even in very cold temperatures. The flow of heat from around your neck, because of the bellows effect when you move, can be minimized by wearing a Head Sokz™ as a "neck dam."

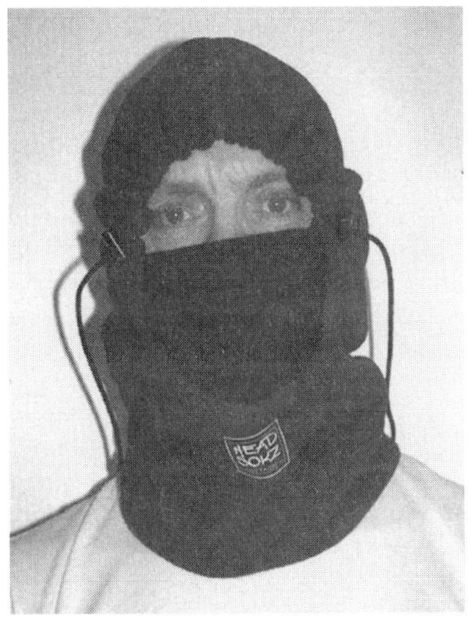

Feet

Keeping your feet warm involves three components: boots, socks, and gaiters. The first step in selecting boots for use in cold weather is to figure out what kind of terrain you will be traveling in, the expected temperatures, whether the conditions will be dry, wet or snowy, and how you will be moving around (snowshoe, walking, riding a horse, ATV, etc.) Pick a boot that meets the requirements for the conditions you expect to encounter, but recognize that no one boot can satisfy all conditions. Check out Schnee's Boots of Bozeman, Montana. They make a very good line of both mild and cold weather boots. Like the rest of your body, the first layer

covering your feet should be a material that wicks water away from your skin. Once again, synthetics, wool or a wool-synthetic mixture should be selected – NOT COTTON! Gaiters worn over your lower leg and covering the upper portions of your boots will also help to keep you warmer and dryer. Another option is boot blankets - insulated over-boots that are put on over your hiking boots as soon as you are no longer moving. Chemical heat packs can also be inserted between the blanket and your boot for increased warmth.

When all things are considered, the act of putting on and taking off clothing in order to adapt to changing environmental conditions is a much easier task than building a fire or an emergency shelter. Lacking appropriate clothing, the survivor must resort to trying to build a fire and erecting a shelter to maintain their body temperature – a task that may prove impossible!

"You cannot make up for inadequate clothing using fire and improvised shelter."

10

Here's What I Carry ... and Why I Carry It!

"It may be more important that you know what does not work than what does."

During nearly forty-five years of wandering around the world's backcountry, I have developed a collection of equipment that has frequently saved my bacon! Equipment that, on more than one occasion, changed a potentially life-threatening situation into an inconvenient night out. Some would call my collection of gear a "survival kit." The mountain men of the Rocky Mountain West would call it a "possibles kit." I call the collection "my emergency gear" and have it with me wherever I go. After all, what good is your emergency kit if you don't have it with you?

Over the years, the contents of my kit have changed. As new equipment came along that was better and lighter than the gear I used, it replaced the old. Despite the changes in the individual pieces of equipment, the categories of equipment I carry have not changed – there are those *must have items;* there are those pieces of equipment that would be *greatly missed* if they were not available; and then there are those pieces of equipment that *you would like to have* with you, but, if you didn't, the world would not come to an end. While it's hard to justify carrying equipment that doesn't get used often, there is some equipment that has to be carried for that once in a life time situation when your fate hangs in the balance – these core items include shelter, fire making, and signaling equipment.

IN MY POCKETS

Some things just belong in your pockets – a folding knife, for example.

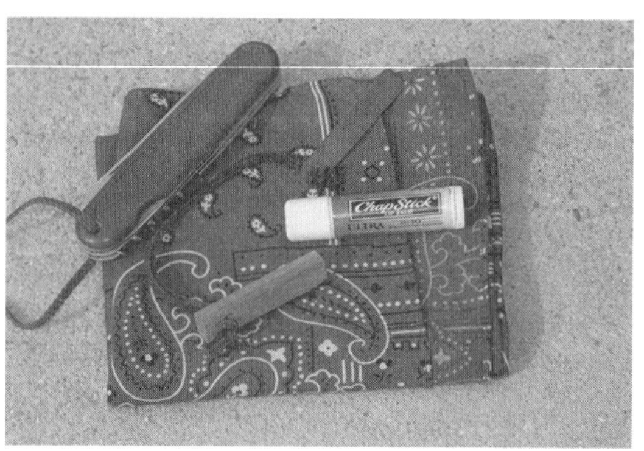

A bandana handkerchief - a piece of equipment that has a thousand uses would be another valuable item. Chapped lips are a constant aggravation – carry with you one of the lip balms with an SPF factor of at least 15 and use it often. I would always have a metal match with me with which to start a fire. Carry those things in your pockets that you need quickly and use often. Then, because of circumstance, if you were separated from all of your equipment bags, you would at least have a few basic items with you that you could use to save yourself.

IN MY GET-AWAY BAG

This bag should contain the emergency gear that you would heavily depend on if you were

stranded, if you were hurt and couldn't make it back, or if you were caught out after dark or trapped by bad weather where continuing on would be dangerous. This bag would usually be carried in your day pack and then removed if the larger pack was left behind. Fundamentally, this bag should contain a waterproof, windproof shelter (material that you could crawl into or crawl under to keep yourself dry and warm), reliable fire starting tools, and the means to signal your distress.

Here's a list of what I carry in my get-away bag:

- 1 heavy duty, 4 mil., orange plastic bag (38″ x 65″) for shelter *
- 1 metal match with scraper*
- 2 match cases* - fill one with REI Stormproof ™ matches and the other with Vaseline saturated cotton balls
- 1 glass signal mirror*
- 1 plastic whistle*
- 1 small folding knife
- 1 orienteering compass
- 1 plastic water bag
- Small stick of pitch wood for fire starting
- 1 small LED light with a head band
- Nylon line
- Chemical hand warmers

* This equipment, packed in a bright orange Cordura® zippered pouch with belt loops, is available from *www.outdoorsafe.com.*

IN MY DAY PACK

In addition to the items listed above, I carry the following additional equipment which might be considered *nice-to-have,* but I could do without even though I might not want to:

- Dandy saw with 17″ blade or Florian® pruning shears
- 18″ x 18″ closed cell foam sitting pad
- 150′ parachute cord dyed red
- Hygiene kit (toilet paper, wipes bar of soap, and jell handsanitizer
- Sawyer Broad Spectrum Mosquito/ Insect Repellant (depends where I'm going – summer only)
- Bug Out Jacket (depends where I'm going – summer only)

- Basic medical kit (band aids, ace bandage, 4 x 4 gauze pads, Imodium® AD tablets, Benedryl® tablets, Bayer's aspirin, Rolaids®, finger nail clipper, dental floss, prescription antibiotic, personal prescription medications
- HeadSokz™ for head protection
- Helly Hansen® Guide raincoat and bibs
- Light leather goat skin gloves
- Synthetic mittens
- Esbit fuel tablet stove with plenty of fuel tablets
- Map of the area
- Chunk of pitch wood for fire starting
- Food bars, cup-of-soup powder, hot chocolate powder
- One quart Nalgene wide mouth, water bottle
- 4 AA batteries, Princeton Tec® flashlight with elastic headband
- 3.5″ Kellam knife Model M571 fixed blade knife.
- One bottle (50 tablets) Potable Aqua® tablets
- One metal cup
- An additional orange DOT plastic bag
- Additional insulated clothing

The ability to produce a lot of firewood quickly makes carrying a

good quality saw a priority. Select a saw that is multi-purpose. The Dandy Saw I carry cuts wood, snow and bone. It is tough, requires no

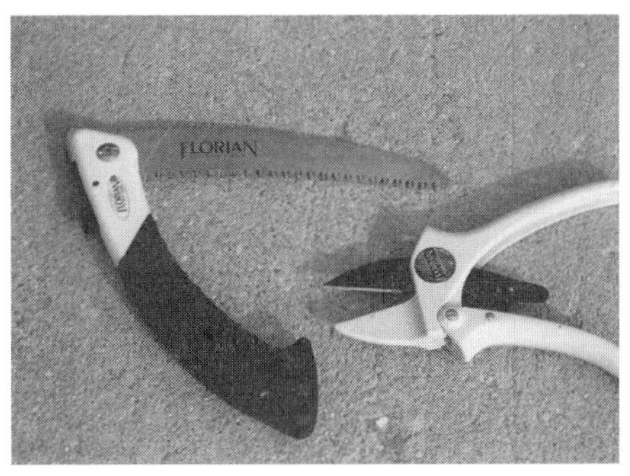

assembly, and has no moving parts. The Florian® folding saw and pruning shears are two other efficient, safe and reliable tools for gathering fuel.

I carry a closed cell foam pad to insulate myself from the ground when I sit down. It also helps to keep my clothing clean and dry. Its most important value may be the padding it provides when I sit on hard ground, rocks or other uncomfortable, cold objects. Parachute line is very useful and will serve as your hammer and nails when you build shelters, line for hanging equipment, sewing thread, dental floss, fishing line and hundreds of other uses. Buy white parachute line from a military surplus outlet and then dye it red or orange (RIT® fabric dye) – a color you can see! Your toilet kit should have "wipes" in addition to toilet paper. Under field conditions toilet paper doesn't do the job well enough. Wipes are the field replacement for a shower or bathtub!

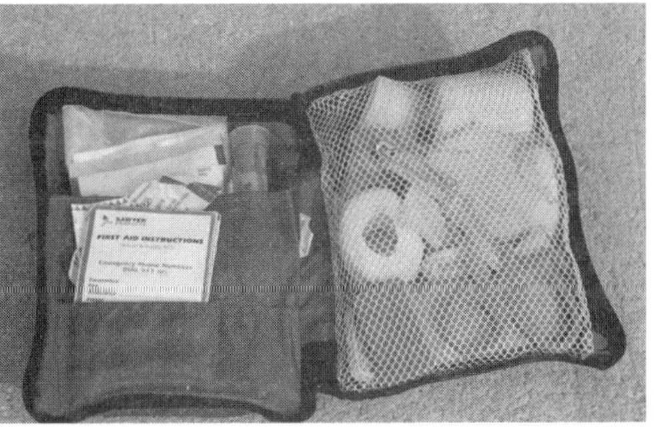

Assemble a medical kit sufficient to handle the commonly encountered medical issues - not to perform major surgery! In the event of a serious injury there is little that those present can do beyond taking the normal first aid steps and then making the patient as comfortable as possible before going for help. Limit the drugs you carry to those personal medications you must have and then add Benedryl for dealing with any allergy issues, aspirin for pain control and for its usefulness when treating someone who is experiencing cardiac problems, and finally Imodium® or other anti-diarrhea medication.

In some parts of the country protection from biting insects is essential. Black flies, deer flies, mosquitoes and other forms of "flying teeth" make life miserable for a survivor and can become a life threatening issue. Head nets, bug-shirts and repellents are virtually impossible to improvise – have them with you when you need them!

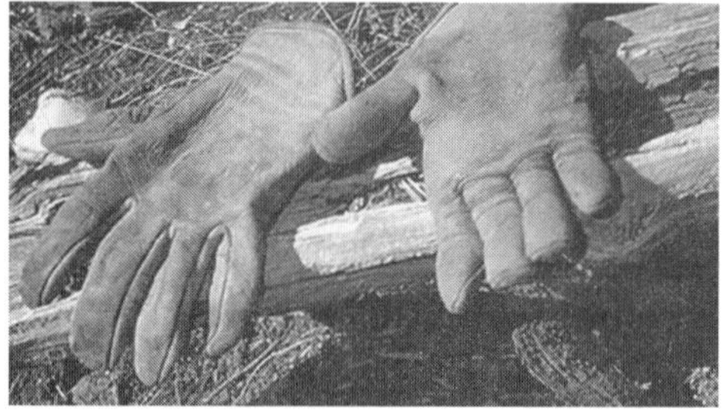

Emergency clothing should include a pair of light leather gloves. Your hands are not as tough as you think they are and will soon become bruised, burned and battered. In colder weather, include mittens in your gear. With functioning hands, survival is difficult. Without the use of your hands, survival becomes impossible. Take care of them. The ability to start a fire under adverse conditions is fundamental to surviving especially when clothing is inadequate and shelter hard to come by. Relying on primitive fire-making skills in the absence of a metal match or good matches is asking for a cold night out and the possibility of becoming a hypothermia victim. An Esbit stove is a very useful device that makes getting a hot drink easy without having to build a fire.

Signaling devices range from expensive electronic devices that can reach out from any location in the world by satellite and make contact with rescuers, to simple less expensive equipment that may not have the range of the more sophisticated gear but can still get the job done. Every emergency pack should, at the very least, contain a whistle and a mirror. Both can be used to attract the attention of ground searchers and, in the case of the mirror, can also be used to signal a passing aircraft or boat. The human voice is a poor signaling device – it doesn't last very long nor does it carry very far! Carry a whistle – it can be blown all day and the blast carries much further than your voice.

Depending on the time of year, other things may show up in my gear. During the colder months, I add a Wiggy's Sweater. This lightweight jacket is insulated with Lamalite, one of the best synthetic insulators available.

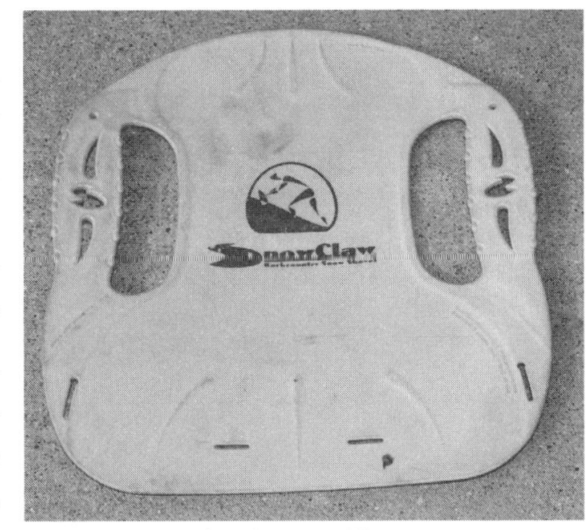
The Snow Claw

Should I need to dig a snow shelter or move snow for any other reason, I add a Snow Claw digging tool. This inexpensive mini-snow shovel works far better than digging with your hands or another improvised shovel and can be used for a number of other purposes as well! In arid regions, I would add additional water containers.

To some of you, this may seem like a lot of equipment to carry around the mountain. To others, it may seem barely enough. We each have to decide what we need based on our circumstances and the situations that we might find ourselves in. Granted, few people are going to find themselves in a survival situation, but when they do, it would be nice to be well equipped, clothed and prepared.

11

The Fork In The Road – To Travel Or Not To Travel

"Experience is not what happens to you – it is what you do with what happens to you."

We arrive now at "the fork in the road" where you, the "survivor," will have to decide whether or not it is in your best interest to remain where you are and allow search and rescue (SAR) forces to find you or to attempt to make your own way back – in essence, "rescue yourself!" For the survivor, this is a critical point in their survival experience. The following issues should be carefully thought through:

- ***Does anyone know you are missing?***

  If you left a "trip plan" with friends or family members, and you did not deviate from the plan, a search will begin as soon as the trip plan expires and the authorities are notified. If someone knows you're missing, you can take heart in the fact that SAR forces will be looking for you. Your job as the survivor then is twofold: to keep yourself alive until they get there and to expedite your recovery by drawing their attention to your location by signaling. If you have not left a trip plan and no one knows where you are or when you are supposed to return, making your own way out may be your only choice. Leaving a trip plan and sticking to that plan is without question your best option for a quicker rescue. Page 123 provides more detail on developing trip plans.

- ***Has your trip plan expired?***

  If you get into trouble before your trip plan expires you may, once again, have to attempt to get back to safety without outside assistance. No one is going to come looking for you until your plan expires! The alternative is to make camp and wait until your plan expires and the SAR forces come looking for you. Remember that since no one is actively looking for you while you wait for your plan to expire, it may be difficult to attract the attention of those that pass by – they are not aware that someone is overdue and are not actively looking for a person who is missing. The moment your plan expires and the search begins, any flash of light, column of smoke or other signal will be investigated and your chances of being seen and rescued significantly improve.

- ***Physical condition***

  You are in your best physical condition as you begin your survival experience and, from this point forward, your physical condition will continue to deteriorate over time. In particular, reduced amounts of water and food will quickly decrease your body's physical and mental efficiency – particularly its ability to regulate your body temperature and to traverse rough terrain safely. People grossly overestimate their physical condition and have little awareness of the difficulties of backcountry travel. Stay put!

- ***Distance to destination***

  People also grossly overestimate their ability to travel and grossly underestimate distance – a potentially-fatal combination! In the heat of the moment, when the desire to be back with family and friends is almost overwhelming, commonsense goes out the window! When the weather worsens and a light in the distance beckons, commonsense once again takes a back seat to the desire to "get out of here!" It is very easy to become a victim of our overconfidence in our ability to effectively travel from one point to another. When in doubt, sit tight!

- ***Weather conditions***

  Traveling when the weather conditions threaten your safety makes no sense! Many have died from exposure to the elements when they continued to move across country in cold (or hot), wet, windy conditions with inadequate protective clothing. Traveling during inclement weather significantly increases the chances of an accident happening. While some survivors have died when they waited at the scene of the crash for rescue to arrive, a great many more died while trying to walk to safety.

- ***Amount of clothing available***

  Lacking the necessary clothing to keep warm and dry increases the likelihood that you will move when the more appropriate action would be to build a fire, erect a shelter and remain in place. Your clothing provides the only shelter you can count on and it should be selected carefully based on its capacity to protect the wearer in adverse conditions and allow you to stay in one place awaiting rescue

- ***Navigational skills***

  The ability to navigate with a map, compass and GPS receiver greatly increases the survivor's ability to travel and the likelihood that they will try to make their own way out rather than wait for rescue. With a compass or a GPS receiver in hand, it is easy to convince yourself that you can find your way back and get out of your predicament. Unless you are totally confident in your ability to navigate successfully, unless you have a specific destination in mind, and unless you are physically able to reach that destination – stay put! When traveling across country, not only do you have to be able to navigate successfully, you also have to continue surviving. It is much easier to maintain your life in a "campsite" environment than it is when you are constantly moving. It is also much more difficult for rescuers to find a "moving target" than it is to find a stationary one!

- ***Amount of survival equipment available***

  Those who find themselves in an emergency are more likely to try to return to safety under their own power if they lack basic survival equipment. On the other hand, those who are equipped and clothed and those who decide that spending the night out is in their best interest will do so knowing that they are prepared, and while it may not be comfortable – it is survivable!

- ***Amount of water and food available***

  The quantities of water and food available play into the survivor's decision to "stay" or "go." Lacking either and knowing that they are available elsewhere is often enough motivation for the survivor to try to move to a location where both water and food can be found. It is appropriate to move short distances to obtain water, but it is not appropriate to travel any distance to obtain food. The impact of reduced water intake can have a serious, immediate impact on the survivor's ability to function. The lack of food will, over time, reduce a person's energy level, but, in the short term, the physiological need for food is much less important than the need to keep hydrated. Most people can live for many days without food – some have lived weeks and months!

- ***Expectations of others***

  Of all the reasons that cause people to move when they should be staying in place, the desire to be reunited with loved ones is probably the most dominant. This desire can be both a powerful catalyst to continue to fight for one's life or it can be the phenomenon that causes a person to attempt to return to their families and friends and die when they might have survived had they resisted that desire and remained where they were.

- ***Promises made to others***

  We tell our spouses we'll be back in time for dinner. We assure our employers that we'll be there ready to go to work in the morning. The promises we make are verbal commitments, commitments that can cause a person who should remain in one place to continue to move. We don't want to cause others to worry. We feel obligated to live up to these verbal contracts that we make and so we continue to move. Break these promises! Your immediate safety is more important than a dinner commitment or showing up for work on time! Break these promises. Hole-up. Wait for better conditions. Wait for daylight. Wait for the SAR forces to find you!

- ***Embarrassment and humiliation***
  These are two powerful psychological phenomena that cause people, especially men, to keep moving on in hopes of finding their way back when they should have made camp for the night, waited for conditions to improve and rescue to arrive. No one likes to admit that they got lost, but it is better to face the situation head on. Accept the fact that you are lost and make the necessary preparations to spend a night out. Embarrassment and humiliation are survivable! Exposure to the elements for lack of adequate shelter may not be!

So there you are, a long way from camp at the end of a day standing at the fork in the road trying to decide which way to turn. The weather looks ominous - it is threatening to snow, the wind is picking up and the temperature is dropping rapidly as the sun sets. It is obvious that it will be dark long before you could reach camp. Your emotions are telling you to keep moving - maybe you'll find the trail, the camp, your car. On the other hand, your commonsense and training are telling you to sit tight, shelter yourself, wait for daylight, the weather conditions to improve or rescue to come. At that moment, only you can decide what the best course of action to take is. Give yourself a chance. (Remember the "STOP" acronym discussed earlier.) Search and Rescue (SAR) personnel across the country will tell you that your chances of survival are much better if you sit tight and let them come and get you than they are if you try to make it back to safety yourself. They would much rather bring you out alive, cold, hungry and tired, but alive, than to bring you out wrapped in a body bag!

Instead of continuing on, you decide that the best course of action is to find a sheltered place and survive! This decision to "sit tight" will not come easily. The thought of a cold night away from your warm sleeping bag, hot food and the camaraderie of friends will be a powerful catalyst for you to try and make it back. Knowing that the other members of your camping party will worry when you don't return will also tempt you to keep moving. The decisions to hole-up for the night comes easier if you have equipped and clothed yourself properly and if you and the other members of your group have discussed what should be done if one of the party does not return at the end of the day.

- ***Look for a "hole-up" site***
  Take the wind conditions into account first. By getting out of the wind, you eliminate or reduce the "wind-chill" factor and are now dealing with ambient (still) air temperature. The difference between the two can be many degrees. The difference between the two can be life saving! While you are looking, put your back to the wind – do not stand facing the wind where the boundary layer of warm air protecting your face is quickly blown away. Look for a barrier that you can get behind – a large tree, a big rock, anything that blocks the wind. Move to the lee side of a ridgeline. Move into the timber. Look for a site that provides you fuel for a fire. Select a location that is safe.

- ***Enhance your "hole-up" site***
  Scrape any snow away from the ground. Level the area where you will sit or lay down. Remove any potential threats to your safety.

- ***Shelter yourself quickly***
  Getting out of weather conditions that threaten your ability to stay warm is your primary concern at this moment. Once your clothing becomes wet, your ability to stay warm becomes very questionable. Remember: "It is much easier to stay warm than it is to warm-up after becoming cold." Remember, too, that your clothing is the only shelter that you can count on to protect yourself. In hot, arid regions, getting into shade or creating shade as quickly as possible is a high priority. Having a plastic bag to crawl into or a tarp to crawl under expedites creating shelter and reduces the importance of finding a natural refuge.

- ***Summarize the situation***
  Gather your thoughts, evaluate the situation, and identify resources that may be available, develop a plan of action and then implement that plan. Once protected, you have bought yourself some time.

When looking at the survival "big picture," there are only three things that must be done in order to keep yourself alive:

1. You must have taken care of any life threatening medical issues that resulted from the event that precipitated you into the situation or that developed while waiting to be rescued.
2. You must be able to maintain your body temperature at 98.6° F.
3. You must be able to keep yourself hydrated. None of these will be possible if you "lose your head," so perhaps it should be said that there are four things that should be done to survive.

12

Emergency Shelters

"It is impossible to build a wind proof, water proof shelter."

If we are to believe the survival manuals and the "how-to-survive" articles published in the popular outdoor press, building a shelter from natural materials in an emergency should be a piece of cake! After all, look at all the trees, bushes, bark and other natural materials you have to work with! Based on what we read, there should always be a convenient hollow tree, rocky overhang or cave a person in trouble could use for shelter. It's strange how when you are not in trouble, any number of suitable shelters can be found, but when you really need one, they are in short supply. Another one of Murphy's laws!

I have always believed that if you are going to need a shelter you had better have the materials with you to build it! I also believe that it is impossible for the survivor to build a waterproof, windproof shelter from natural materials! Some of you may take issue with that statement, but consider this: When do survivors first realize that they need a shelter? Usually when the realization first hits that they are going to have to spend a night out that they hadn't planned on. It's late in the day (maybe even dark already!), the temperature is dropping, the wind's picking up, and it's beginning to rain! This is not the time to be scrambling around the countryside trying to find the natural materials to build your home for the night, especially if you are injured! Have you even wondered how you would build a shelter from natural materials if your arm was broken? Shelters made from natural materials require time, natural resources, a cutting tool is helpful as is a fully functional survivor who has practiced building survival shelters in the past! These commodities are often in short supply in an emergency! The survivor needs a waterproof, windproof shelter now! Being able to protect yourself from inclement weather quickly is a fundamental requirement if you are to survive.

Mylar® Space Blankets And Bags

Mylar® space blankets are light weight, inexpensive, compact and largely USELESS in an emergency! Again consider the scenario I laid out earlier – it's late in the day, cold, rainy, windy and the survivor is injured or hypothermic or both! Space blankets are difficult to get out of the package, they are difficult to unfold and drape around yourself – especially if you are one-handed in a windy situation! They are usually too small for an adult and require the use of both hands to keep you enclosed within the blanket. When enclosed in the material, they are very noisy which might preclude you from hearing the rescuers.

Mylar® plastic tears very easily if nicked or punctured. Bags made out of the same Mylar® plastic are also available; however, other than the fact that they are a "bag," these devices suffer from all of the same flaws that blankets suffer from. I do not recommend products made from Mylar® plastic for emergency shelters.

Thermal Blankets

Thermal blankets are similar to space blankets, but are made from heavier material reinforced with fiberglass threads and with grommets in each corner. Thermal blankets can be used as a body-wrap, but, once again, depending on the size of the person, they are often too small to completely protect an adult. Some survivors have attempted to use a thermal blanket as a shelter roof by tying lines to each corner and stretching the blanket between various anchor points. In benign conditions, this may work, but in windy conditions or with snow loading, the grommets pull out very quickly and the blanket is destroyed.

Tube Tents

Tube tents are another emergency shelter option. Tube tents are generally eight feet long and provide a tubular shelter three feet to five feet high when erected depending on the brand. Tube tents can also be pulled over the body to provide a quick shelter from the elements or they can be used as a "pup tent." To erect a tube tent shelter, tie off a line to an anchor point (a tree), run the line through the length of the tube tent and tie it off to second anchor

point. The tent is then spread out along the length of the line. The height of the horizontal line above the ground should be such that the tent can spread out enough to accommodate the occupant. The plastic that tube tents are made from comes in a variety of thicknesses. With one popular brand, the plastic is only 1 mil thick which tears very easily. In order to withstand the abuse and better meet the needs of a person having to spend the night out, the thickness of the plastic should be at least 3 mils thick – 4 mils is better. Tube tents can be improvised from large household trash bags by opening up the closed end of one bag, sliding it into the open end of the second bag and then duct taping the seams together, as pictured above.

Tarps

Sheets of Visqueen plastic, painter's drop cloths, canvas or other similar materials can be used to erect a wide variety of effective survival shelters. "Blue Crinkly" tarps are readily available, inexpensive products from which emergency shelters can be quickly built. These tarps can be purchased from most hardware stores, come in a variety of sizes and are usually blue on both sides with grommets in each corner and at intervals along the sides. An eight foot by ten foot tarp is large enough to provide sufficient protection for an adult. Tarps of this size weigh about 26 ounces and can be rolled up into a tube six inches in diameter by 12 inches long, which makes them very convenient to carry on the outside of a daypack or fanny pack. Tie 10 feet of parachute line to each corner grommet before you go outdoors to expedite erecting the shelter when time is short.

Tarps can be erected in a number of styles depending on the weather conditions that the survivor is exposed to. To erect a lean-to tarp shelter,

first select a line long enough to stretch between two trees that are far enough apart for the tarp to be stretched tight. Using a Timber Hitch, (*see next page)* tie off one end of a line to an anchor about chest height, then, rather than passing the line through the grommet eyes, insert a bend in the line through the grommet eye and place a short stick through the eye in the line (*see next page*) . Repeat this process for each grommet stretching the tarp tight each time. With the tarp attached to the line, tie off

the other end of the line to the second tree, again stretching the line as tightly as possible. The lower edge of the tarp is then pegged to the ground or anchored with large stones or a length of log.

When making pegs, select a length of wood 1½ to 2 inches in diameter and twice as long as is needed. Using a saw, make one 45° cut at the mid-point of the stick. In this way, one cut produces two pegs both of which are sharp enough to drive into the ground using a mallet.

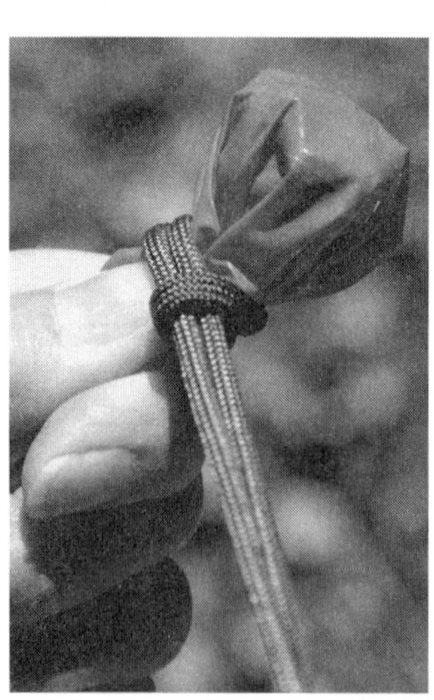

If possible, orient the shelter so that the lower edge points into the prevailing weather; however, if a fire is to be used to heat the lean-to, the front of the shelter should be parallel to the prevailing wind. Oriented in this manner, the wind will carry the smoke away from the shelter rather than into it.

When using material without grommets, use improvised buttons instead of cutting a hole in the tarp to attach a line. A small, smooth pebble, pine cone or similar object is placed under the material and bunched up as shown in the accompanying picture on page 100. Using a Girth or Clove Hitch, attach a line to the "button" that is created. This method of attaching a line to a tarp is much stronger than tying a line through a hole cut in the fabric and will not tear out as quickly.

Plastic Bag Shelters

Large, heavy grade (3-4 mil) orange plastic 55 gallon drum liners make good short-term emergency shelters. It may be difficult to warm-up and dry out after becoming cold and wet and, consequently, you need a shelter that you can crawl under or, better still, crawl into quickly when weather conditions deteriorate. A large plastic bag serves this purpose very well. Totally encapsulating yourself inside a plastic bag is not a good idea. Apart from the need for oxygen, the water vapor contained in the air you exhale and your perspiration will condense on the inner surfaces of the bag and the occupant can get quite wet.

To minimize this problem cut an opening in the closed end of the bag just large enough to allow you to pass your head through. The bag is then passed over your head until your face aligns with the hole and the moist air is exhaled to the outside. When creating the hole, cut the plastic along a seam about five inches below one corner. Cut at ninety degrees to the fold to reduce the likelihood of the bag tearing

along the seam. The hole should be just big enough to pass your head through when you are getting too warm and need to cool down.

Being able to protect oneself from the onslaughts of the weather is a fundamental survival skill. Not to do so is an invitation to dying from hypothermia! Too many people venture into the outdoors without carrying a shelter or the materials to make a shelter thinking that they will be able to build one from whatever natural materials they find. Many of these same people find out too late that it is very difficult, if not impossible, to build a windproof, waterproof shelter from natural materials. They also find out that the clothing they are wearing may be adequate when they are active, but is totally inadequate when they are stationary. Sheltering, i.e., defending your body core temperature from dropping below 98.6° F, begins with selecting appropriate clothing. With good clothing you may not need any other shelter. With inadequate clothing, you had better have something in your gear to protect yourself from precipitation, wind and temperature extremes. Inadequate clothing places a premium on your ability to find or construct a shelter and on your ability to build a fire. In the final analysis, the only shelter you can count on is the shelter provided by your clothing. Pick it carefully! The only heat that you can count on is the heat your body is producing. Don't waste it!

13

Fires And Fire Building

"Fire, the greatest of man's discoveries, enables man to live in many climates, use many kinds of foods, and compels the forces of nature to do his work."

Jack London's famous story of the dog musher who dies in the Arctic because of his inability to keep a fire going still serves as a vivid reminder of how quickly things can go wrong when we fail to take into account all of the pitfalls we face when building fires under emergency conditions. The situation is worsened when the sources of information we go to for guidance do not provide information that can be relied on to help in an emergency. The nonsense that is written about "how to start a fire" is a case in point.

In *Camping and Woodcraft,* authored by Horace Kephart and published in 1906, the author speaks of starting fires by "striking flint, quartz or pyrites a glancing blow with the back of a knife or piece of hard steel" to produce sparks. He talks of using "the lens of a camera, field-glass, or telescope" as a burning glass to start a fire and then goes on to explain how "a watch crystal, removed, and then three-fourths filled with water, forms a lens that, if held very steadily, will ignite punk or tinder," It is interesting to note, and herein lies the crux of the problem, that in the latest Bradford Angier book, *Basic Wilderness Survival Skills,* published in 2002, the same fire starting procedures are discussed! They must have been remarkable woodsmen to have been able to build their fires using these methods! I maintain that these procedures could not have been relied on for emergency fire starting in 1906 or in 2002, and they are not methods that can be relied on today. Easier, more practical methods that work reliably under adverse weather conditions must be learned.

Most commonly, the need for a fire does not arise until some crisis is at hand. The weather has become life threatening; a person has fallen into the river and needs to be re-warmed quickly, a hunter needs a fire to stay warm when faced with spending a night out far from camp, or other similar circumstances. These are not the times to get your first practice at building a fire! It is advisable to get that practice in your backyard the next time the rain or snow is falling. That is the time to practice and determine the strengths and weakness of the fire starting equipment you carry and the soundness of your fire building skills. If either the equipment or the skills come up short, you can retreat to the safety of your house and re-think both while warming up.

The sources of heat you carry to start your fires must be easy to use when your hands are cold and have lost their dexterity. The devices must function every time regardless of temperature, altitude or precipitation. The amount of heat supplied must be long lasting and since survivors are often injured the devices should still function with only one hand.

Matches

Many different types of matches are available. Unfortunately many are of poor quality and are designed not for use in the field but for lighting cigarettes and other uses around the home.

• *Safety Match*

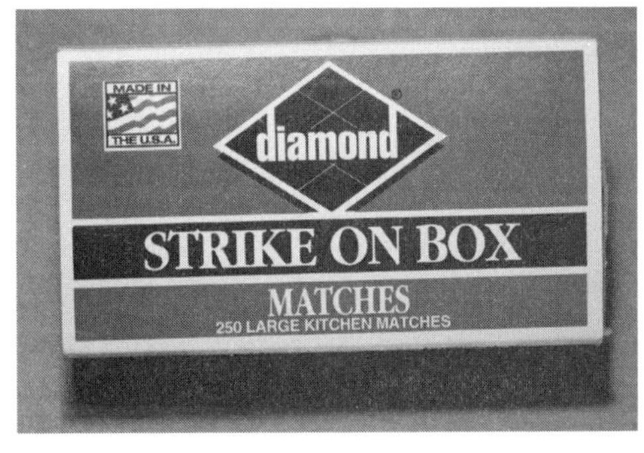

In order for a match to light, the chemicals on the match head must be combined with the chemicals on the striking pad in the presence of oxygen. Safety matches are designed to be ignited by striking the match head on the striking pad on the box *from which they were removed!* A match taken from one box may not light by striking it on the pad of another match box. The chemicals are different.

• *Waterproof Matches*

These matches have been dipped in a waterproof lacquer that is water resistant when it dries. In order to light a waterproof match, the match head must be struck against the striking pad repeatedly until the lacquer is worn through and the match head chemicals can come in contact with the chemicals on the pad. For some matches, this may only take a strike or two, but, with others, many strikes are required to ignite the match. With every strike, the pad becomes more contaminated with the waterproofing material and, eventually, a point will be reached where you still have matches but the pad is so contaminated that it no longer works. Some waterproof match boxes only have a striking pad on one edge of the box making a bad situation even worse! For this reason, I do not recommend waterproof matches. I do recommend placing good matches in a waterproof container, however.

- ***Windproof Matches***

These matches usually have a bigger head than normal matches, both in terms of the length and the thickness of the match head. Once again, these matches can be difficult to light under benign conditions and almost impossible in adverse weather. Some, once lighted, only smolder with little if any flame.

- ***Strike Anywhere Matches***

These once readily available matches are becoming more difficult to find. They can be identified by their two tone heads - usually blue and white, green and white or red and white. Both chemicals needed for combustion are combined on the head of the match. The term "strike anywhere" would lead you to believe that they could literally be "struck anywhere". Nothing could be further from the truth!

These matches must be struck on the striking pad or on material that is just abrasive enough to light the match and yet not so abrasive that the match head is ripped off. Such a surface can be difficult to find when the ground is covered in snow! While some people have developed the skill to ignite strike anywhere matches on the seat of their pants or by flicking the match head with a thumbnail or even using their teeth, these methods of igniting strike anywhere matches are not reliable in an emergency. Always have a piece of the striking pad with you.

• *Stormproof Matches*

Stormproof matches are usually water resistant and do not blow out in windy situations. Here, again, it pays to test these matches before committing them to your emergency gear. Some are much better than others and the best of them all are the stormproof matches sold exclusively by Recreational Equipment Incorporated. (REI). With these matches, as long as the match head material remains, they cannot be blown out, even in very windy conditions. If extinguished in water, they will relight when removed. I encourage you to replace any matches you currently carry with REI Stormproof ™ matches! Your life may depend on it.

Match Containers

All matches should be carried in a waterproof container that is easy to open one-handed. Here again you have choices to make.

• *Boy Scout Style*

This kind can be very difficult to open when your hands are cold and stiff and have lost their dexterity. Boy Scout style match cases are impossible to open one-handed and can be very difficult to open if grit gets into the threads.

• *Military Style*

With the exception of the color, OD Green, the military style case meets all of my criteria for a good match container. It is tough, waterproof, and easy to open one-handed. OD Green match cases can be hard to find if dropped in the grass! A small piece of metal match is embedded in the base of the case. Scraping this with a sharp edge produces sparks which can be used to ignite tinder. A popular misconception is that this material is used for striking a match.

• *Orange Military Style*

These match cases are available in most sporting goods stores where they are usually sold under the Coghlan's trademark. These are orange versions of the military style match case and, while they are not quite as sturdy, they are the match case I use. This type of case comes in two lengths with the longer of the two just long enough to accommodate the REI matches. If the shorter version is used, the REI matches must be trimmed before they are placed in the case. When filling a match case with REI matches, place half the match heads down and half with the match heads towards the top which allows more matches to be carried in the case. A piece of the striking pad must also be inserted in the case making sure that when you do so the striking surface is placed towards the plastic wall away from the match heads.

• *Multipurpose Match Case*

This popular match case should be avoided. The device, which includes a whistle, a mirror, a small piece of metal match, a compass and a match case, combines all of these survival tools into one which, on the surface, sounds like a good idea. The problem arises when the device is lost or damaged. Should this happen, it is possible to be without a means to start a fire, navigate or attract attention to yourself. It is better to buy the individual pieces of equipment and not put all of your eggs in one basket.

Other Methods of Igniting Tinder

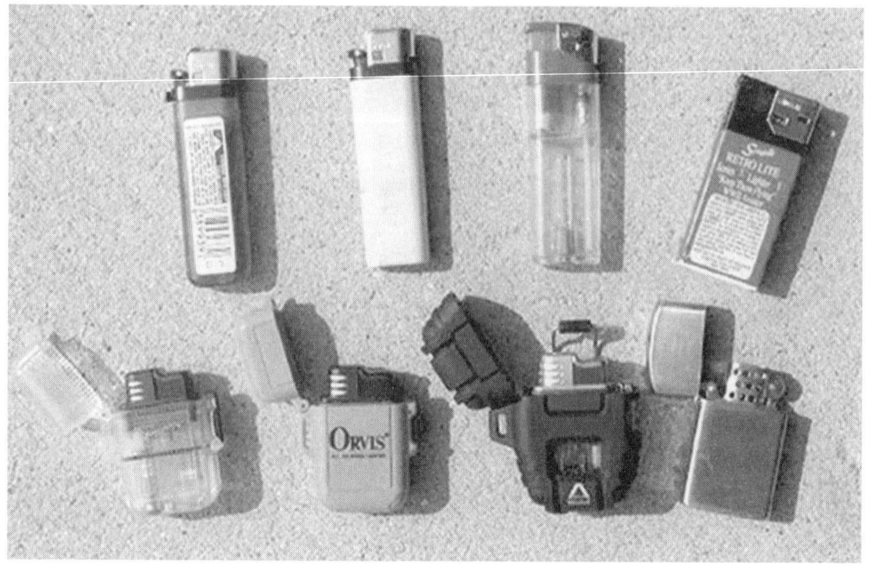

Cigarette lighters are frequently carried by those who are unaware of their shortcomings. Consider the following:

- ***BIC® Style***

These are pressure sensitive (the higher the altitude the less the fuel will vaporize), and temperature sensitive (the colder the temperature the less the fuel will vaporize). They will explode if accidentally dropped into a fire, and they require good hand dexterity to operate, which isn't a problem when it's warm but quickly becomes a problem in cold conditions.

- ***Zippo Lighters***

These have one significant advantage over the BIC® style which continues to burn only as long as the fuel release remains depressed. Once lit, a Zippo lighter will burn as long as the cover is not replaced. One disadvantage of these lighters is that the fuel tends to evaporate rather quickly.

• *Piezo Ignition Style Lighters*

These lighters use an electronic spark to ignite the fuel similar to the spark produce by a BBQ lighter. This system is much easier to use than the BIC® style requiring far less finger and hand dexterity. If you are going to carry a cigarette lighter, select one with a piezo-ignition mechanism and a clear fuel reservoir. If out in cold conditions carry the lighter in an inner pocket where it will stay warm.

• *The Colibri Quantum™ Lighters*

These are more expensive devices that are alleged to be waterproof, shockproof, windproof and will ignite at higher altitudes. Field testing of these lighters does not show this to be the case.

Metal Matches come in all shapes and sizes. The material used to produce the sparks is very similar to the "flint" used in a BIC® lighter, only much larger. Some metal matches are imbedded in a block or cylinder of magnesium which can be scraped with a sharp metal edge to produce magnesium shavings. By scraping the metal match with a sharp edge, a shower of sparks can be created with which to ignite tinder. Magnesium shavings are difficult to keep together in windy conditions, burn very quickly, and are not recommended as a primary heat source for building a fire in an emergency. There are other types of tinder available that ignite easier and burn longer. The best of these is a mixture of household cotton saturated with Vaseline discussed later in this chapter.

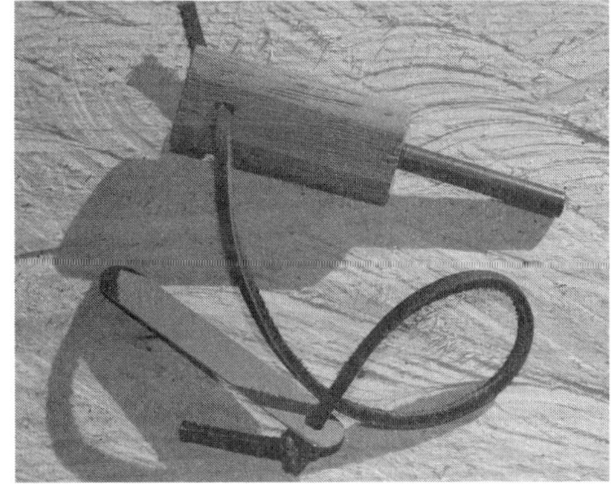

When faced with choosing the best fire starting device and

comparing the fire starting potential of a metal match versus a box of matches, the metal match wins hands down. In a test I conducted, over 500 fires were started using the metal match shown. Compare this with a typical box of matches, which contains 25 – 30 matches. For most people, more than one match, sometimes many more, will be needed to start a fire. A metal match should be a fundamental part of every survival kit.

Building Fires

When the need for a fire is critical, not only must the tinder light easily, but the steps used to build the fire must quickly result in a self-sustaining fire, every time, regardless of the weather conditions. This is often easier said than done, but much can be learned that will make your fire building efforts more successful.

Keep in mind that, for a fire to burn, three elements are required: a heat source sufficient to ignite the tinder is necessary; oxygen must be available; and good quality fuel must be on hand. When building a fire, remember, too, that it's not the wood that burns, it is the flammable gases contained within it that ignite. The amount of heat provided by the heat source, the metal match, match, or cigarette lighter,

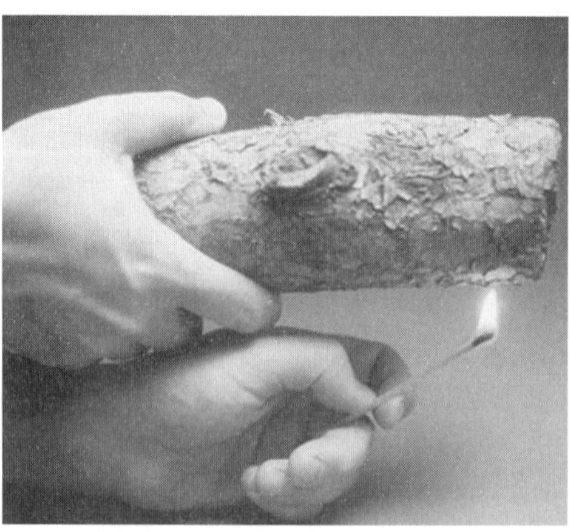

must be hot enough to drive off the flammable gasses contained within the tinder. Then the heat provided by the burning tinder must, in turn, drive off the flammable gasses contained within the larger fuel. One of the most common mistakes made by inexperienced fire builders is trying to light fuel that is far too large for the amount of heat that is available to light it – the heat is insufficient to produce the gasses needed for combustion to occur.

Step number one in building a fire is collecting the fuel to be burned. Too often I see people picking up sticks from the ground and, while you might get by doing this during the heat of summer, this fuel will seldom burn well at other times of the year when rain and snow saturate any wood that is lying on the ground. Whenever possible, it is better to collect your fuel, especially that which will be used in the early stages of the fire, by snapping off the dead branches found under overhanging tree limbs. The moisture content of this wood will be far lower than that collected from the ground. If the wood bends rather than snaps, it is probably green – don't use it. If there are green leaves or needles attached to the branch, discard it – it won't burn! The small dry dead branches found under the overhanging branches of fir and spruce trees are particularly good for the early stages of a fire.

Gather far more fuel than you expect to need. Having accumulated a substantial pile of fuel, separate the wood into three piles by size. The first pile should be match-stem thick or thinner. The second pile should be sticks up to the thickness of your thumb, and the third pile

should be made up of all the fuel that remains.

When the ground is wet, it is advisable to assemble a platform of sticks, approximately one foot square, to protect the tinder. If the tinder is placed directly on the wet ground, it tends to absorb moisture from the soil which may make it more difficult to light.

If small sticks to make this platform are not available then they must be made by splitting large sticks into smaller pieces using your knife and a mallet. Splitting wood in this manner also exposes the dry inner surfaces of the wood which can then be used as fuel when other dry fuel is not available.

Vaseline™ - Cotton ball Tinder

Of all the tinders that are available, both natural and man-made, a cotton ball saturated with Vaseline™ works the best under a broad range of conditions. Fluff-up a cotton ball, make sure it's cotton not synthetic, and smear in large quantities of Vaseline™ until there is little or no dry cotton left. The cotton serves as a wick and the Vaseline™ becomes the fuel. This mixture should be placed in a screw top container until needed. When needed remove a cotton ball, fluff it up again by spreading the fibers apart and ignite with the sparks from a metal match.

Wind will have a dramatic effect on your fire building efforts, especially when trying to ignite tinder. To provide the best chance of your tinder igniting and continuing to burn, place a short log, about 10 to 12 inches long and about 4 inches in diameter, along the windward side of the platform. Place the tinder in the lee of the log where it is protected from the wind. When trying to build a fire in rainy conditions or when the snow is falling, find a sheltered area out of the precipitation or erect a temporary roof over the fire site to shelter the tinder until the larger fuel is burning.

Before you light the tinder you must have everything ready. The second most common mistake made by inexperienced outdoors men and women is that of igniting the tinder and then finding they haven't prepared the next stages adequately, whereupon they have to scramble around trying to find more materials to add to the rapidly burning tinder. Before the first match is struck or the first spark is produced by your metal match, arrange the kindling so that it is in easy reach.

With all in readiness, place the tinder on the platform in the lee of the windbreak and then ignite it. As soon as the tinder is burning, a handful of the smallest fuel is placed over the flames with one end

of the twigs resting on the log brace. This will only work well if you have resisted the urge to break the twigs into short pieces – another common error made by those new to fire building! The fuel used in building a fire should be broken into lengths 10 to 12 inches long. Resting one end of the twigs on the brace ensures that good airflow is maintained and the tinder is not smothered when additional fuel is added - another very common mistake. If you have to blow on your fire, something is wrong with your selection of fuel or your fire building process!

As the twigs begin to burn and the flames appear through the first layer of fuel, lay a second handful of twigs over the first layer, but this time lay them at 90° to the first. As the flames appear above this layer, place another handful of slightly larger twigs on the fire again at 90° to the previous layer. This process continues until the larger fuel has been added and the fire will sustain itself without the immediate attention of the person building it.

The success of building a fire using this method is contingent on using tinder that produces a lot of heat, ensuring good ventilation, and graduating from the smallest twigs to increasingly larger sizes of fuel gradually.

Throughout this description of fire-building, the term "build" a fire has been used as apposed to the commonly used phrase "start a fire." Other fire building procedures are advocated in the popular outdoor press and literature devoted to "bush craft!" Many of these techniques recommend assembling the entire fire structure from tinder stage to the larger fuel and then lighting the tinder contained within the structure. It is my experience that this procedure very often leads to failure when the tinder fails to ignite the next stage of the fuel and the entire structure must be dismantled and then rebuilt before trying again. Far more success can be achieved by using the procedure outlined above where you light the tinder and each layer begins to burn before you place the next. Should a problem arise and the tinder fail to ignite the first stage of fuel, the structure can be easily rebuilt.

When building a fire is debated, the SAFE use of petroleum products should be included in the discussion. The methods commonly used are not safe and frequently result in damaged equipment and clothing, at best, and, at worst, personal injury. Fuel, red gas, white gas or any other similar petroleum products should **NEVER** be poured over a pile of sticks and then ignited. The result of this is usually an explosion and injury to the bystanders!

Instead, the fuel should be poured into a shallow container – the bottom two inches of an aluminum soda container work well. The fuel vapors on the surface are lit with a match or a cigarette lighter. By using this procedure, only the fuel vapors on the surface of the fuel ignite – there is no

explosion! The fuel will continue to burn until it is expended. Once the fuel is burning, sticks can then be placed over the burning fuel which, in turn, will begin to blaze. Using fuel this way is safe and particularly useful when trying to ignite damp or even wet wood under adverse conditions – the burning petroleum will dry the wood. Care must be taken to ensure that, when adding wood to the fire, that the container holding the fuel is not upset. Should this happen, the fire will flare and injuries could result.

Before building any fire, careful consideration should be given to the ensuring that the fire does not escape and cause an even bigger problem for the survivor. Select a site that is free from materials that could inadvertently catch fire and carry the flames to other inflammable materials. It is wise to scrape away any ground cover that might catch fire. Be careful when building a fire under overhanging vegetation which could ignite. During the winter months, fires built under snow covered branches will usually result in a cascade of snow into your fire. Either shake the snow from the branches before building a fire or select another safer site. Building a fire during windy conditions where sparks could escape the immediate fire site should be avoided if possible, but if it is still necessary to build the fire, select a protected site out of the wind. Placing a log on either side of the fire will also help to contain a fire from spreading. When no longer required, a fire should be completely extinguished. Dousing the fire with large quantities of water is usually the best way to do this, but for those situations where water is not immediately at hand, mixing the coals with earth until no hot embers remain is the next best method.

14

Getting Yourself Rescued – to be seen or not to be seen!

"You can never count on help. You can only count on not getting help."

The single most important step in getting rescued quickly is to leave a trip plan with two reliable people that you can count on to raise the alarm when you don't show up on time. Two people are better than one because, as luck would have it, the one person you are depending on to raise the alarm forgets when you are due to return or is ill that day and doesn't alert the authorities! It follows then that having left a trip plan, you must abide by it and, if you should decide to deviate from the plan, you must inform those with whom you left the original plan.

The trip plan should include the following information:

- Names and ages of the members of the party
- Color, make, model and license plate number of vehicles used to transport the group to the departure point
- Departure point

- Return point if different from the departure point
- Date of departure and return
- Equipment and clothing carried
- Experience level of the group
- Medical histories of those with known medical conditions
- Unusual medical conditions of any member of the group
- Location of planned campsites

This information should be written on the back of a copy of the topographical map you will be using. On the map mark your departure point, your route of travel and the dates and locations of the places you expect to overnight. Maps can be downloaded from several online sites which make it easy to leave the information needed by rescuers to find you quickly.

The rescue process begins when you fail to return on time and the alarm is raised by those in possession of your trip plan. Calling 911 is usually the first step. The operator receiving the call will alert the agency responsible for searching for missing and overdue people and a process begins that should ultimately result in your recovery. Depending on the part of the country you live in, search and rescue (SAR) operations are the responsibility of the county sheriff, local Fish and Game agents or other law enforcement agencies working with volunteer SAR organizations. SAR organizations, working under one of the lead agencies listed previously, are manned by volunteers who are trained, equipped and totally committed to search for and recover missing people. Other agencies, including the military, the Coast Guard, and the Civil Air Patrol, can become involved particularly when specialized equipment is needed to find the survivors or to recover them from particularly difficult terrain. Assuming that a trip plan has been left, you can take comfort in the fact that an organized process exists and is being employed to find and recover you from your predicament.

Without a trip plan, the process becomes vastly more complicated. To begin with, someone has to become aware that you are overdue! You are not at work, you failed to return home for dinner and you haven't called your Mom lately! Once someone is aware that you are missing, the process of trying to determine your whereabouts begins. This is usually a combined effort of local law enforcement officials, family members and friends, and involves a lot of detective work. Where you were last seen? Who did you talk to? What was said that might shed some light on what you were planning to do or where you were planning to go? Once your departure point has been established (often by locating your car), the search area narrows and SAR forces, which may include both ground and airborne assets, can be deployed to try to find you. Your job as the survivor is twofold. First to survive! To maintain 98.6° F. for as long as possible, to keep yourself hydrated and to treat any injuries as best you can thereby giving the SAR forces a chance to recover a grateful, living survivor. Secondly, to make yourself more visible so that you can be found quickly.

Leaving a trip plan is the most important step you can take to get yourself rescued quickly. The next most important step is to remain in one place and wait for rescuers to arrive. It is very difficult for those trying to find you if you are constantly moving or, as one rescuer put it, "It's hard to hit a moving target!" So be patient, sit tight and make yourself more visible.

How to Be More Visible

- ***Electronic aids:*** ***(Beacons, cell phones, family radios, etc.)***

Electronic signaling devices are wonderful when they work and have resulted in the rapid recovery of many people in trouble. Some things to keep in mind: They are line-of-sight devices. I.e., if the device cannot "see" a microwave or cell phone tower or, in some cases, a satellite because of terrain, dense vegetation or other obstructions, you will be unable to establish a communications link. Secondly, they are subject to malfunctioning and battery depletion. Thirdly, there have been instances where the survivor was talking by radio or cell phone with SAR personnel but, because of weather, rough terrain, distance or other factors, recovery was still hours, perhaps days away. You will still have to survive until they get to you!

Pay attention to surviving and let the rescuers worry about finding you and getting you out! All electronic devices should be considered aids to getting you found and recovered, not an excuse to leave your survival equipment at home. As of July 2003, Personal Locator Beacons transmitting on 406 Megahertz are available that, when activated, transmit a unique, personalized signal to a series of satellites that down link the signal to rescuers who can then home in on your precise whereabouts. Similar devices such as Emergency Personal Indicating Radio Beacons (EPIRBs) and Electronic Locating Beacons transmitting on 121.5 MHz are being phased out and will no longer alert authorities if deployed after February 2009.

- ***Light producing devices***

For night time use handheld strobe lights, laser lights, flashlights, flares, and Chem-light sticks are all readily available. Utilizing modern electronic search gear and night vision equipment any light source, including that of a fire can be detected. Other equipment carried onboard search aircraft can even detect your body heat.

For day time use a commercial glass signal mirror is one of the best means of attracting the attention of rescuers. I have seen the reflected light from a 3 x 5 inch mirror 26 miles away! Signal mirrors made from metal and plastic are also available, but they do not have the brilliance of a good glass mirror. Mirrors can be improvised from any shiny material that may be available, including CD-ROMs and even the hologram on a credit card, but, once again, the brilliance pales when compared to a glass mirror. Select a glass mirror that incorporates an aiming mesh which enables the user to precisely aim the mirror. If you are with a vehicle do not overlook the rearview mirrors or the headlights as possible ways of attracting attention.

Inexpensive emergency road flares available from most auto parts stores make very good night time signals. They are long lasting and will continue to burn even in bad weather. (They are also good for starting fires in damp weather) The light produced by three separate fires is also a recognized emergency signal.

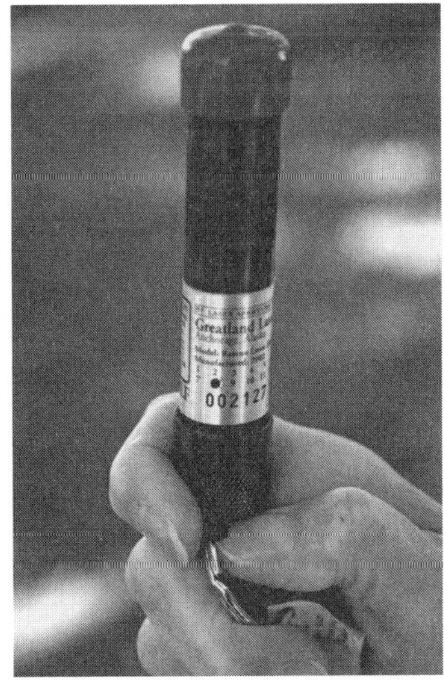

Laser lights specifically designed for signaling are available. These hi-tech signaling devices produce a beam of light that lengthens as it travels further away from the source rather than a "spot" of light commonly seen with classroom laser pointers. Laser lights are capable of being seen up to 20 miles away, although its effective range is less than that. The light, when directed at a nearby surface, may only be a foot long but the same beam of light has lengthened to 3,600 feet when viewed from a rescuer ten miles away! To use the device, first locate the target, usually a search aircraft seen only by its lights, and then slowly sweep the beam of light back and forth across the target. Any part of the light beam, which is not harmful to the viewer, appears as a brilliant, distinctly different red flash to the rescuer. A laser light could be considered the night time equivalent of a signal mirror.

• *Noise producing devices*

A good plastic whistle should be included in everyone's emergency gear. Unlike your voice, which gives out quickly when you are yelling, a whistle can be blown all day long. It does not require great skill to operate and can be used one handed! Blow the whistle in a series of three blasts with a lengthy pause, several minutes, between each series to listen for rescuers who will respond with one long blast. Keep blowing the whistle until the rescuers place a hand on your shoulder.

Shots fired from a firearm are usually not good signals, especially if fired in daylight hours during the hunting season. At other times of the year or if fired after dark, the sounds of gunshots can be useful in locating a survivor. Traditionally, shots fired in a series of three are an indication that someone is in trouble. If gunshots are to be used successfully to signal for help, those who hunt together should decide not to fire any shots until a predetermined, designated time after dark. Because gunshots tend to echo, it may be difficult to pinpoint their origin. However, hearing the shots confirms that someone is in trouble. It is at this time that initial contact should be made with the authorities responsible for conducting search and rescue so that they can begin their preparations to commence a search early the following morning. Postponing contact with SAR personnel until the following morning delays the beginning of a search by at least eight hours!

• *Ground to air symbols*

Unlike the previously discussed signaling devices, once constructed, symbols laid out on the ground in geometric form do not require the active involvement of the survivor to be effective. Build them and leave them! While there are many symbols that can be used to communicate a specific message, it is only necessary to erect something that catches the eye of the SAR personnel. A large cross is sufficient. SOS still works! ANY mark or disturbance will be investigated once the search begins. To be effective, when building symbols, incorporate straight lines, sharp angles and good color contrast. If possible, symbols should be situated in a large open area where they can be seen by an aircraft approaching from any direction.

A useful commercial product for attracting the attention of rescuers both on land and water is a Rescue Streamer™. This device consists of a 25 foot long, 6 inch wide, orange ribbon that, when deployed,

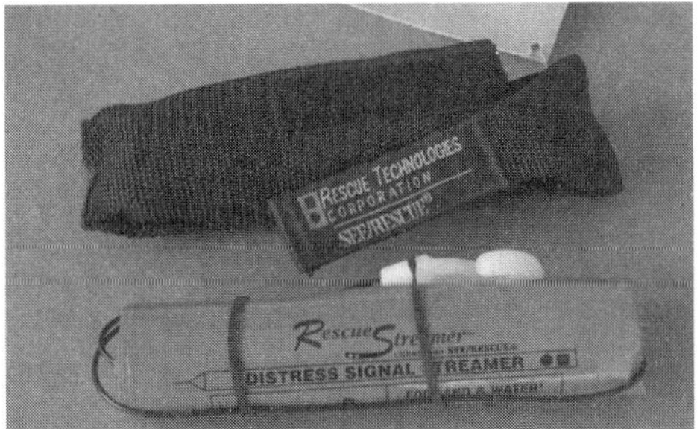

creates a vivid signal that contrasts well against a wide variety of backgrounds. Weighing only 5 ounces and packaged in a holster that clips to a belt, the Rescue Streamer™ is an effective signaling device for attracting the attention of rescuers. An added advantage, unlike pyrotechnics and battery operated devices which have a finite operating life, these signaling devices last indefinitely

• *Smoke*

A column of smoke rising high into the air is easy to see from an aircraft flying over the search area and may also be visible to ground search teams. Elaborate structures are not necessary to produce large columns of smoke and neither are three fires placed in a triangle as advocated in most survival books. Building and maintaining three separate fires requires a significant expenditure of energy and then, once alight, the columns of smoke tend to consolidate and form one column anyway.

In preparation for an approaching aircraft, the survivor should have collected a large pile of highly flammable materials and an even larger pile of green vegetation. Upon hearing an aircraft approaching place the flammable materials onto the existing campfire and, as soon as they are burning, place the green vegetation on top. Allow the fire to get going before placing the green vegetation on the flames. The hotter the fire, the greater the amount of smoke that is produced. It is important that the column of smoke is produced as the aircraft is approaching – smoke rising after the aircraft has passed by will probably not be seen. Green vegetation will produce white smoke. Black smoke can be produced by burning petroleum products, foam rubber from seats and even tires. If inflated tires are used, remove the valve stem or puncture the tire before placing on the fire. Not doing so could result in an explosion and injury from flying, burning rubber!

A few final thoughts. It is very frustrating for the survivor on the ground to be looking up at passing aircraft and wondering why he or she can't be seen. It is equally frustrating for those in the aircraft looking over hundreds of square miles trying to pick out the survivor from the background. Be patient. Make yourself bigger. You will be seen. Keep in mind that an active search will not start until your trip plan expires and someone raises the alarm. Prior to the search commencing, passers by will be unaware that you are overdue and may not react to your attempts to attract their attention. Once an active search begins, any glint of light, discoloration, disturbed area or other possible sign of the missing person will be thoroughly investigated. Keep the faith. Sit tight. Rescue will come.

APPENDIX

Sources for Survival Equipment and Outdoor Clothing

The author of Surviving a Wilderness Emergency receives no financial support from any of the companies listed below. This listing is provided to enable the reader to obtain the equipment referenced in the book. Any recommendations for this equipment made in the book were made based on the author's use of the equipment or clothing.

OutdoorSafe Inc.
P.O. Box 62039
Colorado Springs, CO 80962-2039
719-593-5852
Email: info@outdoorsafe.com
www.outdoorsafe.com

Survival kits and kit components, whistles, mirrors, metal matches, emergency shelters, match cases. Also available is the video, ***Preparing to Survive,*** and the book, ***Surviving a Wilderness Emergency Manual,*** available as printed matter and on CD-ROM.

RavenWear
P.O. Box 411
Caroline, Alberta, Canada TOM OMO
800-387-2836
www.ravenwear.ca
Fleece cold weather clothing, thermal underwear

MPI Outdoors
www.mpioutdoors.com
Orders: 800-421-1223
www.clorders.com/mpiproducts.htm
Esbit® stoves

Berti's Glove Company
P.O. Box 136
Harrison, ID 83833
208-689-3111
www.berti4gloves.com
Leather gloves and other leather products

Greatland Laser
P.O. Box 221407
Anchorage, AK 99522-1407
907-245-4475
www.greatlandlaser.com
Emergency laser signaling devices

Rescue Technologies Corporation
888-411-9888
www.rescuestreamer.com
RescueStreamer® distress signals,
SEE/RESCUE® distress signal streamer

Wiggy's Inc.
P.O. Box 2124
Grand Junction, CO 81502
800-748-1827
www.wiggys.com
Cold weather clothing and sleeping bags;
Lamalite® sleeping bags

Headsokz, Inc.
P.O. Box 1393
La Quinta, CA 92247
800-946-8824
www.headsokz.com
Head protection

Counter Assault
120 Industry Court
Kalispell, MT 59901
800-695-3394
www.counterassault.com
Bear deterrent pepper spray

Outfitters Pack Station
2070 West Broadway
Idaho Falls, ID 83402
800-657-2644
www.outfitterspackstation.com
Cold weather clothing, Helly Hansen rain gear,
Dandy saws

Chinook Medical Gear, Inc.
120 Rock Point Drive, Unit C
Durango, CO 81301
800-766-1365
www.chinookmed.com
Medical supplies, backcountry medical kits,
survival equipment

Wyoming Outdoor Industries, Inc.
1231 13th Street
Cody, WY 82414
800-725-6853
www.wyomingoutdoor.com
Stainless steel cup; Dandy saws

ACR Electronics, Inc.
5757 Ravenswood Road
Fort Lauderdale, FL 33312
800-432-0227
www.acrelectronics.com
Electronic locating beacons; EPIRBs; strobe lights; survival radios

The Original Bug Shirt Company
P.O. Box 127
Trout Creek, Ontario, Ca P0H 2L0
705-729-5620
www.bugshirt.com
Insect protective clothing

Emergency Response International
319 Olive Street
Cashmere, WA 98815
800-353-9953
www.emergencyresponseintl.com
Pre-Mac personal water purifiers

Snow Claw International
877-904-3200
www.snowclaw.com
Snow shovels

Kellam Knives Co.
902 South Dixie Hwy.
Lantana, FL 33462
800-390-6918
www.kellamknives.com
Inexpensive, tough fixed blade knives (M571)

American Standard Company
157 Water Street
Southington, CT 06489
800-275-3618
www.floriantools.com
Florian® Ratchet-Cut® pruning tools, folding saw

Carol Davis Sportswear
P.O. Box 19333
Omaha, NE 68119
712-847-0300
www.cdsportswear.com
High performance, hydrophobic,
antimicrobial thermal underwear

Pak-Lite Company
512 Humberd Lane
Grants Pass, OR 97527
541-660-0349
www.paklite.net
LED flashlight

MyTopo.com
P.O. Box 2075
One South Broadway
Red Lodge, MT 59068
877-587-9004
www.mytopo.com
Custom printed topographical maps printed
on waterproof paper

Lat. 26° Inc.
P.O. Box 511044
Punta Gorda, FL 33951
800-305-0036
www.lat26inc.com
GPS map plotters and other useful navigation equipment

Equipped to Survive™
313 W. Temple Court
Gilbert, AZ 85233-7724
www.equipped.org
Survival equipment and outdoor gear reviews

US Geological Survey
P.O. Box 25286
Denver, CO 80225
888-ASK-USGS (275-8747)
www.usgs.gov
Topographical maps

For Additional Training

Medical Training

Crested Butte Outdoors, L.L.C.
P.O. Box 2802
Crested Butte, CO 81224
970-359-6311
www.cboutdoors.com

Stonehearth Open Learning Opportunities
P.O. Box 3150
Conway, NH 03818
603-447-6711
www.soloschools.com

Wilderness Medical Associates
400 Riverwside Street, Suite A-6
Portland, ME 04103
888-945-3633
www.wildmed.com

Wilderness Medicine Outfitters
2477 County Road 132
Elizabeth, CO 80107
303-688-5176
www.wildnernessmedicine.com

Wilderness Medical Society
810 E. 10th Street
P.O. Box 1897
Lawrence, KS 66044
800-627-0629
www.wms.org

Bibliography

Aitken, Jim. *Take the Survival Challenge*, Arms & Armour, 1990.

Alloway, David. *Desert Survival Skills*, University of Texas Press, 2000.

Angier, Bradford. *How To Stay Alive In the Woods: A Complete Guide To Food, Shelter, and Self-Preservation That Makes Starvation in the Wilderness Next to Impossible*, Fireside, 1998.

Ashcroft, Frances. *Life at the Extremes: The Science of Survival*, University of California Press, 2002.

Auerbach, Paul S. *Wilderness Medicine (Wilderness Medicine: Management of Wilderness and Environmental Emergencies)*, C.V. Mosby, 2001 (4th ed.)

Bezruchka, Stephen. *Altitude Illness: Prevention and Treatment*, Mountaineers Books, 1994.

Bowman, Warren D., M.D., and Bitter, Reata (Illustrator). *Outdoor Emergency Care: Comprehensive Care for Nonurban Settings*, National Ski Patrol System, 3d ed., 1998.

Boy Scouts of America Staff Editors, *Official Boy Scout Fieldbook*, Boy Scouts of America, 1979.

Boy Scouts of America Staff Editors. *Okpik: Cold Weather Camping*, Boy Scouts of America, 1997.

Brown, Tom. *Tom Brown's Field Guide to Wilderness Survival*, Berkley Trade, 1983.

Burns, Bob, Burns, Mike and Hughes, Mike. *Wilderness Navigation: Finding Your Way Using Map, Compass, Altimeter and GPS*, Mountaineers Books, 1999.

Cheff, Sr., Bud and Cheff, Bud. *The Woodsman and His Hatchet: Eighty Years on Back Country Survival*, Stoneydale Press Publishing Company, 1997.

Churchill, James E., *Basic Essentials of Survival*, Ics Books, 1989.

Churchill, James E. *Basic Essentials of Survival*, Globe Pequot, 1999 (2nd ed.).

Cornett, James W. *Indian Uses of Desert Plants,* Palm Springs, CA: Palm Springs Desert Museum, 1995.

Craighead, Frank C., and Craighead, John J. *How to Survive on Land and Sea,* Naval Institute Press, 1984 (4th ed.).

Dubas, Frederic and Vallotan, Jacques, Ed. *Colour Atlas of Mountain Medicine*, Elsevier Science, Health Science Division, 1991.

DeLeo, Peter. *Survive: My Fight For Life In the High Sierras*, Simon & Schuster, 2005.

Duke, Jim and Meuninck, Jim (Director). *Edible Wild Plants; Field Guide to 100 Wild Herbs* (VHS), _________, 1988.

Edholm, O.G. and Bacharach, A.L. (contributor). *Physiology of Human Survival*, London, New York: Academic Press, 1965.

Fear, Gene. *Surviving the Unexpected Wilderness Emergency,* Tacoma: Survival Education Association, 1973.

Fleming, June. *Staying Found: The Complete Map and Compass Handbook*, Mountaineers Books, 2001 (3rd ed.).

Fletcher, Colin. *The Complete Walker III*, New York: Alfred A. Knopf, 1987 (3rd ed. rev.).

Forgey, M.D., William W. *The Basic Essentials of Hypothermia*, ICS Books, 1991.

Forgey, M.D., William W. *Wilderness Medicine: Beyond First Aid*, Globe Pequot Pr., 1999 (5th ed.).

Forgey, M.D., William W., and Ross, James W. (contributor), and Bradfield, Victoria (contributor). *Hypothermia, Death by Exposure*, Ics Books, 1985.

Forgey, M.D., William W., Ed. *Wilderness Medical Society Practice Guidelines for Wilderness Emergency Care*, Globe Pequot, 2000 (2nd ed.).

Fry, Alan. *Wilderness Survival Handbook : A Practical, All-Season Guide To Short-Trip Preparation And Survival Techniques For Hikers, Skiers, Backpackers, Canoeists, Snowmobilers, Travellers in Light Aircraft – And Anyone Stranded In The Outdoors*, St. Martin's Griffin, 1996.

Ganci, Dave. *Basic Essentials of Desert Survival*, Ics Books, 1991.

Ganci, David. *Hiking in The Desert*, Contemporary Books, Incorporated, 1979.

Gonzalez, Laurence. *Deep Survival: Who Lives, Who Dies, and Why*, W. W. Norton & Company, 2004.

Graves, Richard L. *Bushcraft: A Serious Guide to Surviving and Camping*, Warner Books, Inc., 1986.

Grubbs, Bruce. *Desert Sense: Camping, Hiking & Biking in Hot Dry Climates*, Mountaineers Books, 2005.

Harding, A.R. *Deadfalls and Snares*, Fur Fish Game, 1970.

Hare, Trevor. *Poisonous Dwellers of the Desert: Description, Habitat, Prevention, Treatment*, Western National Parks Association, 1995.

Harvey, Mark. *National Outdoor Leadership School's Wilderness Guide*, Simon & Schuster, 1999 (prev. printing, Simon & Sullivan, 1983).

Hodgson, Michael. *Basic Essentials of Weather Forecasting*, Globe Pequot, 1999 (2nd ed.)

Houston, Charles H. *High Altitude Illness & Wellness*, Globe Pequot, 1998.

Jacobson, Cliff. *Basic Essentials of Knots for the Outdoors*, Globe Pequot, 1999 (2nd ed.)

Jacobson, Cliff. *Basic Essentials of Map and Compass*, Globe Pequot, 2005.

Jacobson, Cliff. *The Basic Essentials of Trailside Shelters and Emergency Shelters*, Ics Books, 1992.

Jamison, Richard L. *Primitive Outdoor Skills: More Wilderness Techniques From Woodsmoke Journal*, Horizon Publisher & Distributors, 1985.

Janowsky, Chris and Janowsky, Gretchen. *Survival - A Manual That Could Save Your Life*, Paladin Press, 1989.

Johnson, Mark. *The Ultimate Desert Handbook: A Manual for Desert Hikers, Campers and Travelers*, International Marine/Ragged Mountain Press, 2003.

Kals,W.S. *Land Navigation Handbook: The Sierra Club Guide To Map, Compass & GPS*, University of California Press, 2005.

Kephart, Horace. *Camping and Woodcraft*, Univ. of Tennessee Pr., 1988.

Kirk, Donald R. *Wild Edible Plants of the Western United States*, Headlsburg, CA: Naturegraph Publishers, 1975.

Kjellström, Bjön. *Be Expert with a Map and Compass*, John Wiley & Sons Canada, Ltd., 1994.

Kochanski, Mors L. *Northern Bushcraft*, Lone Pine Pub, 1989.

Leach, John. *Survival Psychology*, New York University Press, 1994.

Lehman, Charles A. *Desert Survival Handbook*, Phoenix: Primer Publishers, 1988.

Lehman, Charles A., Fessler, Diane (contributor) and Smith, Dennis L. (contributor). *Emergency Survival*, Primal Pub, 1980.

Letham, Lawrence. *GPS Made Easy: Using Global Positioning Systems in the Outdoors*, Mountaineers Books, 2003 (4th rev. ed.).

Manhoff, David and Vogel, Stephen N., Ed. *Mosby's Outdoor Emergency Medical Guide: What To Do in an Outdoor Emergency When Help May Take Some Time to Arrive,* Beachwood Healthbooks, Inc., 1996.

Maniquet, Xavier and Roberts, Ivanka. *Survival: How to Prevail in Hostile Environments*, Facts on File, 1994.

McDougall, Len. *Practical Outdoor Survival: A Modern Approach*, The Lyons Press, 1993.

McPherson, John and McPherson, Geri. *Primitive Wilderness Living & Survival Skills*, Sunflower University Press, 1993.

Mears, Raymond. *The Outdoor Survival Handbook: A Guide To The Resources & Material Available In The Wild & How To Use Them For Food, Shelter, Warmth & Navigation*, St. Martin's Griffin, 1993.

Mooers, Robert L., Jr. *Finding Your Way in the Outdoors*, New York: Outdoor Life Books, 1984.

Muston, John. *Survival: Training and Techniques*, Dorset, Poole : New York, NY : Arms and Armour Press ; Distributed in the USA by Sterling Pub. Co., 1987.

Nelson, Dick and Nelson, Sharon. *Desert Survival*, Glenwood, NM: Tecolote Press, 1977.

Nessmuk, George W. Sears, *Woodcraft and Camping*, Dover Publications, 1963.

Nester, Tony. *Desert Survival Tips, Tricks & Skills*, Diamond Creek Press, 2003.

Olsen, Larry Dean. *Outdoor Survival Skills*, Chicago Review Press, 1997 (6th ed.).

Owen, Peter. *Book of Outdoor Knots,* The Lyons Press, 1993.

Peterson, Lee Allen, and Peterson, Roger Torry (illustrator). *Field Guide to Edible Wild Plants*, Peterson Field Guides®, Houghton Mifflin, 1999.

Petzoldt, Paul. *The Wilderness Handbook*, New York: Norton, 1974.

Randall, Glenn. *Cold Comfort: Keeping Warm in the Outdoors*, Lyons and Burford Publishers, 1987.

Risk, Paul H. *Outdoor Safety and Survival*, John Wiley & Sons Inc., 1983.

Saunders, Charles Francis. *Edible and Useful Wild Plants of the United States and Canada*, Dover Publications, 1976.

Schimelpfeng, Tod and Lindsey, Linda. *Wilderness First Aid,* National Outdoor Leadership School, 2003 (3d ed.).

Schneider, Bill. *Bear Aware: Hiking and Camping in Bear Country*, Helena, MT: Falcon Press, 1996.

Scott, David. *Survivalist's Little Book of Wisdom*, Ics Books, 1997.

Setnicka, Tim J. *Wilderness Search & Rescue*, Appalachian Mountain Club Books, 1980.

Shanks, Bernard. *Wilderness Survival*, New York: Universe Books, 1987.

Smith, David. *Backcountry Bear Basics: The Definitive Guide to Avoiding Unpleasant Encounters*, Mountaineer Books, 1997.

Stark, Peter. *Last Breath: Cautionary Tales from the Limits of Human Endurance*, Ballantine Books, 2001.

Stewart, Charles E. *Environmental Emergencies*, Baltimore : Williams & Wilkins, 1990.

Stoffel, Robert and LaValla, Patrick. *Survival Sense for Pilots*, 1980, Emergency Response Institute.

Survival (Army Field Manual: No. 21-76), US Government Printing Office, 1992.

Tilton, Buck. *Back Country First Aid and Extended Care*, Falcon, 2002 (4th ed.)

Torres, Steven. *Mountain Lion Alert: Safety for Pets, Landowners, and Outdoor Adventurers*, Falcon, 1997.

Uman, Martin A. *All About Lightning*, Dover Publications Inc., 1986.

United States Air Force Search and Rescue Survival Training: AF Regulation 64-4, New York: MetroBooks, 1992.

Weir, Ben, Weir, Benjamin M., Benson, Dennis C. (contributor), and Weir, Carol (contributor). *Hostage Bound Hostage Free*, Westminster Press, 1987.

Weiss, Hal. *Secrets of Warmth: For Comfort Or Survival*, Mountaineers Books, 1999.

Wilkerson, Ernest. *Snow Caves for Fun and Survival*, Johnson Books, 1992.

Wilkerson, James A., Bangs, Cameron C., and Hayward, John S. (Editor). *Hypothermia, Frostbite, and Other Cold Injuries*, Mountaineers Book, 1986.

Wilkerson, James. *Medicine for Mountaineering & Other Wilderness Activities*, Mountaineers Books, February, 1993 (4th ed.).

Wiseman, John. *Survive Safely Anywhere-The SAS Survival Manual*, Crown Publishers, 1986.

Survival Stories

Cathy Jacob – June 2005

This story was emailed to me several weeks after the incident occurred.

Dear Peter,

I took two of your classes several years ago with the Wilderness Medical Society in Snowmass CO. (My husband is the doctor). On June 12th I went to the Artic National Refuge in northern Alaska for a 2 week rafting trip down the Kongakut River. It is an indescribably beautiful place. The very last day, a group of us, 4 total, decided to climb the highest peak in the area to see the Artic Ocean. There was too much ice in the river to paddle all the way to the coast, which was our plan. Half way to the top, 2 in the party decided to turn back, so just 2 of us continued on to the top. It was a fairly long distance from camp, about 6 miles. The weather was perfect, not a cloud in the sky etc. Even though we had to cross two ridges and two valleys, the camp was always visible, even though very faint. This as it would turn out caused me to make a huge mistake.

I have always carried your survival kit in my day pack, no matter how short a hike I've taken. On this day, I also had an extra layer of clothes plus rain gear. Because the weather was so nice, I did not use my compass or map to take bearing to the top. The weather turned on us in about 2 minutes after reaching the summit. I have never before experienced a change in weather as drastic. The temperature dropped dramatically. It started snowing and the wind was so strong it was difficult to stand up. I told my companion that we must get off the mountain and start back down immediately. My mistake was that I did not force her to comply. She wanted to stay until the weather cleared a bit so she could see the Arctic Ocean. In a matter of minutes, it became a complete white out. You seriously could not see your hand in front of your face. I immediately realized the danger of the situation. Everything you said in your course came back to me. I found a rocky outcrop that gave us some protection from the wind. I sat down. I kept my head and tried as best as I could to feel my way down and try to recognize any landmarks. In the white out it was impossible to tell direction and even if we were going up or down. The danger, besides the weather, is that the area is just so BIG. If we came down the mountain another side or direction from where we came from, no one would ever have found us. The tundra is so immense and there are no trails. Nothing to indicate which way to go down was the correct way. I got my whistle out and started blowing the SOS signal. I had my compass ready in case the weather cleared enough just for a second to take a reading and I must admit, I prayed. I knew I had the survival "tent" in my pack but I also knew it would be difficult to survive the cold and amount of snow. After about 30 minutes there was the slightest thinning of the clouds. I saw the river far below and was ready with the compass and took a reading. I grabbed the woman's hand and started down, continuing to blow the whistle every minute or two. Although we could not see anything, literally, I kept following the compass. About half way down, I was able to see a tiny speck of yellow, the parka of one of the guides who had come searching for us. They were way off to the left, but I knew then we were safe. I can't tell you what that felt like!!

Peter, there is no doubt in my mind that if I had not had your course, I would still be on that mountain somewhere. It was so hard to remain calm and clear headed. I had to completely focus on staying calm. I thought of my children for a brief second and had to forcibly put them out of my mind because I felt the fear come up through my stomach. I also constantly told myself to think positively. I pushed every negative thought out of my head. I also realize that my skill level was not adequate for this type of crisis. I wanted someone else to take charge and save us. The scariest moment was when I realized that I had to do this by myself or we both were not going to make it. I have never been in a more dangerous situation and it has changed my life. I'm not sure how or if I can thank you enough for saving my life.

Sincerely, Catherine Jacobs

The following story was related to me in Portland, Oregon at the conclusion of a seminar I was giving at the Oregon Sportsmen's Show. The individual involved preferred to remain anonymous so I have used the name "Bob Jones."

> Twenty eight year old Bob Jones was hunting elk in Oregon. Several feet of snow covered the ground and it was snowing lightly. While walking along Bob tripped over an unseen log and fell headlong into the snow. No injuries resulted. Bob got up, brushed off the snow adhering to his clothing, cleaned the snow from his rifle barrel and scope then continued hunting.
>
> Several hours later heavy snow began to fall and Bob decided to return to his truck. Reaching into his pocket for his GPS receiver he was horrified to find it gone. Bob was depending on his GPS receiver to get him back to his vehicle. Other than the clothing he was wearing he had no additional clothing. Since he was confident in his ability to return to his truck he carried no survival equipment. With heavy snow falling Bob began to walk hoping that the direction he had chosen would bring him back to his truck. With every step he took his confidence ebbed away and he soon found himself running blindly through the forest in total panic.
>
> In total panic he raced along when suddenly a thought penetrated the panic that prompted him to ask "What would Peter do?" Reflecting back on a seminar I had given several years previously that he had attended he remember my advice to people in this circumstance "Sit down. Get off your feet. You can't walk if you're sitting on your butt!" Bob found a log and sat down. Thinking back on the program he asked "OK.

What would he do now?" "Have a drink of water. Eat something." Bob drank some water and ate a candy bar. As I had taught in that seminar and subsequently in many others, Bob sat there for thirty minutes allowing the adrenaline that had flooded through his system to subside and for his head to clear. Thirty minutes later he drew a map in the snow at his feet and realized that he was running away from his truck - not towards it. Picking a new heading he started towards the road and an hour later arrived at the road and shortly after that found his truck.

In Bob's words "Had I not remembered what you taught me "Sit down, have a drink, stay there for thirty minutes I would not be alive to tell you this story."

Roy L. Allen – Oct 2004

Sam and I went elk and deer hunting off the SW coast of Washington near the mouth of the Columbia River. Sam borrowed his father-in-laws 20 foot cabin cruiser. Our plan was to live off the boat and shuttle back and forth in my 10.5 foot long inflatable dory using oars. The area surrounding the island is tidal mud flats that are exposed at low tide for a great distance from the island so to reach the island one had to be mindful of the tides and consult the tide book frequently.

We arrived in the area about 3pm on the 9th of September with a plan to stay five days. The weather was "California" nice. We moored the boat to a lone piling in the water about 200 yards from the shore. When we awoke at 5am the next morning the boat had a side ways tilt to it and was not rocking to any waves. Sure enough we were resting on the mud flats at low tide. We had no way to get to the island until the tide returned to a sufficient depth for my inflatable dory to float. Hunters are cautioned that it is too dangerous to walk across muddy tide flats. Even if we had tried to walk ashore we would have been confronted with a 20 foot wide, waist deep slough to wade across. We finally got ashore at about 10 am with the sun shining and the temperature about 70 degree plus.

After hunting all day Sam and I met about 7pm on the bank above the dory. The wind was way too strong to row against it to get back to the boat. With daylight fading rapidly we started building an emergency shelter and collect some dry tinder and fuel for a warm fire. Sam did not bring any rain gear with him ashore for the day had been so nice. He did have a black trash bag that he put on over his camouflage tee shirt and under his leaf net camo jacket. I had regular rain gear that I donned at the first drop of rain at 3:15pm. We used the inflatable dory as the roof to our shelter. I cut boughs with my folding saw to enclose the back and sides. We caught rainwater off the roof to fill our empty water bottles. The tinder was too damp to get the fire started. Sam asked if I had any fire starter. I said no. I said that I had made some tinder by saturating cotton balls with petroleum jelly which I had put in some plastic film cartons. However I did not remember bringing any. Then I decided to look in the orange emergency kit bag that I had bought at one of the Hunter Sportsmen's Show from Peter Kummerfeldt and OutdoorSafe, Inc. Peter had demonstrated to my son and I how hot and long this cotton and petroleum jelly mixture would burn. So when I got home I made some up to put in my hunting gear. Sure enough I had put two of them in this orange bag! So Sam "the master fire builder" went to work and with 1 and ½ plastic cartons worth of fire starter had a roaring fire going in the rain.

So Peter your petroleum jelly and cotton worked like a charm and we used the orange trash bags as our ground cloth. However, our shelter was on about a 2% grade that prevented us from sleeping stretched out parallel under the length of the inflatable boat as our roof and we would slide downhill off the slick plastic bag towards the fire. Since we had rain gear and rubber boots to cover us from waist down, we slept with our lower torsos sticking out into the wind and rain.

With best regards - Roy

P.S. My order for additional plastic bags is attached.

Robert Jevons – 2005

I met Peter at the Wilderness Medical Society meeting in Aspen last summer. The very next day I used the orange plastic bag shelter when caught in a sudden downpour on a hike up Castle Peak, Colorado.

THANKS -

Bob

PETER KUMMERFELDT

Peter grew up in Kenya, East Africa and came to America in 1965 where he joined the U.S. Air Force. He is a graduate of the Air Force Survival Instructor Training School and has served as an instructor at the Basic Survival School, Spokane Washington, the Arctic Survival School, Fairbanks, Alaska, and the Jungle Survival School, Republic of the Philippines. He also served for twelve years as the Survival Training Director at the United States Air Force Academy, Colorado Springs, Colorado. He retired from the Air Force in 1995 after 30 years of service. In 1992, concerned with the number of accidents that were occurring in the outdoors each year he started the Survival Consultant Group and later OutdoorSafe Inc. and has since addressed over 20,000 people as the featured speaker at numerous seminars, conferences and national conventions. His efforts have reduced the number of people becoming injured, ill or dying in the outdoors each year and have heightened traveler's safety awareness especially when traveling overseas.

Peter has been featured on many television programs including "Roving with the Practical Outdoorsman," "The Outdoor Edge." "Oklahoma Outdoors and The Outdoor Guides." Numerous newspapers and magazines have featured him as an authority on outdoor safety and survival. Peter has also participated in many radio shows where he provided current, accurate timely information to many thousands of listeners.

Today he is renowned for his informative programs, his highly developed speaking skills and his ability to work with federal, state and local government agencies, as well as numerous civic organizations, schools and other groups interested in receiving quality wilderness safety training. Peter is currently on the faculty of Emergency Response International. He is an active member of the Outdoor Writers Association of America. He is a Life Member of the Rocky Mountain Elk Foundation, the Dallas Safari Club, Safari Club International, the Rocky Mountain Bighorn Sheep Society, the International Hunter Education Association and the National Rifle Association. Peter has also worked as a licensed fly fishing guide in Colorado and New Mexico and as a big game guide in Colorado and Wyoming.

For seminars, lectures, workshops, field courses, corporate training on outdoor safety, survival in arctic, desert, tropical or temperate regions of the world and travel safety contact:

OutdoorSafe, Inc

www.outdoorsafe.com

Email at: info@outdoorsafe.com

or call 719-593-5852

Notes

Notes

Notes

Notes

Notes

Notes

For seminars, lectures, workshops, field courses, corporate training on outdoor safety, survival in arctic, desert, tropical or temperate regions of the world and travel safety contact:

OutdoorSafe, Inc

www.outdoorsafe.com

Email at: info@outdoorsafe.com

or call 719-593-5852